HUNTING FOR FOOD

GUIDE TO HARVESTING, FIELD DRESSING AND COOKING WILD GAME

JENNY NGUYEN + RICK WHEATLEY

Published by

LIVING READY *fw*

Living Ready, an imprint of F+W Media, Inc.
700 East State Street • Iola, WI 54990-0001
715-445-2214 • 888-457-2873
www.livingreadyonline.com

To order books or other products call toll-free 1-800-258-0929 or
visit us online at www.shopdeerhunting.com and livingreadyonline.com

Cover photography by
Dustin Reid and Jenny Nguyen

ISBN-13: 978-1-4403-3842-7
ISBN-10: 1-4403-3842-6

Cover Design by Sharon Bartsch
Designed by Dane Royer
Edited by Chris Berens

Printed in China

10 9 8 7 6 5 4 3 2 1

Dedication

With deep love for our parents Alice, Hanh, Joe and Ho, who put up with us.

Acknowledgments

Special thanks to Ben Rutten and Kim Rutten Schilousky for their generous knowledge on snapping turtles and crayfish; Aaron Phillip Schroder, hunt guide and dog trainer at Pheasant Bonanza Hunt Club (NE), for being such a great friend; Terry Bisgard for good times in the duck blind; Scott Wessel and Josh Kounovsky for always thinking of ways to help; Gary Bottger for being a better dove hunter than we are; Nick Tramp for being an invaluable resource; John Hundahl of Hundahl Deer Hunts (NE) for lending us a hand when we needed it most; Ngoc Nguyen for his graphic work; Jeff Borchers for his gift of Canada geese; our favorite journalist Mark Davis at the *Omaha World-Herald* for spreading the word; *NEBRASKAland Magazine* Editor Jeff Kurrus for his patience and enthusiasm; and the Nebraska Game and Parks Commission staff for their support and expertise.

Table of Contents

CHAPTER 1   **DEER** 6

CHAPTER 2   **WILD HOG** 24

CHAPTER 3   **RABBIT** 40

CHAPTER 4   **SQUIRREL** 50

CHAPTER 5   **WILD TURKEY** 62

CHAPTER 6   **QUAIL** 78

CHAPTER 7   **DOVE** 90

CHAPTER 8   **PHEASANT** 100

CHAPTER 9   **WATERFOWL** 112

CHAPTER 10 **GAME FISH** 130

CHAPTER 11 **TURTLE** 146

CHAPTER 12 **FROG** 160

CHAPTER 13 **CRAYFISH** 166

Introduction

This book won't teach you how to shoot the biggest buck. This book won't teach you how to catch the biggest fish. Instead, it was written to show you how to hunt and catch something that you can eat, and to allow you to reconnect with the past while providing you with skills and knowledge that you may be able to use in the future. Whether you have never picked up a fishing rod, gun or bow before, or you have been doing it for years, *Hunting for Food* is a reminder of what hunting and fishing is about at its most basic level: Hunting and fishing game for food allows us, as people in a modern world, to never grow dull to the knowledge that food, life and death are all connected. Just as important, it is also about holding onto the freedom of knowing how to provide and to do things on our own.

In these pages, you will learn the basics of hunting and catching many different species of game and fish, and you will also learn how to properly care for each species in the field to maximize your experience at the dining table. Field dressing and butchering directions are shown with step-by-step photos, and cooking tips and recipes are included at the end of each chapter. Once you get beyond the cleaning and butchering part, cooking will be a cinch. Wild game is not scary and anyone can learn how to cook it. Wild game is also very delicious – forget what anyone has ever told you about it tasting "gamy," "fishy" or "tough." If you've had it before and didn't like it, give it a second chance and do the hunting, fishing, butchering and cooking yourself – the right way. You may be surprised by how much of a difference it makes.

We hope that the information in this book will serve to empower and humble, which was our experience while writing our blog *Food for Hunters*, which then led us to write this book. From all the preseason preparation, to hours and days of sitting or searching, to actually shooting or catching something and gettting it out of the field, going through the intimate process of gutting and butchering the animal, and then cooking and eating it – is a revelation. You will learn to see, know and appreciate food in an entirely different way, and we are really excited for all the new hunters and fishermen who will take to the fields and waters to begin this journey.

Every fall we sportsmen leave our homes. We arrive in our blinds and treestands before the rising of the sun and sit for hours in the cold and quiet, listening to the hooting of owls. The hours we will spend watching squirrels will make up much of our lives, and more often than not, we will come home with nothing. But we don't mind – for no one knows the song of the wind that chimes through the trees, or the swelling and receding currents of grass in the fields like we do. To watch the sun peep over the horizon and spill its color into our woods and onto the twinkling surface of our marshes is a privilege and a pleasure. To be given the opportunity to come home with hard-earned game, is a gift.

White-tailed deer antlers have single tines that grow from the main beams, while mule deer antlers have forked tines.

CHAPTER 1

DEER

There are few icons more recognizable in hunting than that of the deer hunter. From primitive cave paintings, to the elaborate medieval tapestries in the halls of the European elite, to portrayals in children's movies, deer hunting is a loaded concept, a familiar motif in history, politics, art and popular culture. Consequently, out of all North American game, deer hunting also suffers greatly from a long festering sin of preconceived notion.

For too many, the hunting of deer is not only questionable, but its meat is often falsely classified as second-rate. As hunters, we've heard all the prejudices, even from within our own ranks. "It's gamy." "It's too tough." "It smells." To this we say, rubbish! In our house venison is the favored game. Unapologetically delicious, organic and ethically killed through the spirit of self-reliance and respect, venison is everything grass-fed beef wishes it could be, and more.

Biology

The two most hunted species of deer in North America are the white-tailed deer and mule deer. Their physical differences can be seen in the ears, tail and antler formation. Mule deer get their name from their long mule-like ears. The antlers on a mule deer will fork as they grow from the main beams, whereas the white-tail's rack has single (not forked) tines that grow upward from its main beams. The tail on a mule deer has a black tip and is narrower than the tail of the white-tailed deer. Both species have excellent senses of smell, eyesight and hearing, a combination that makes them very challenging to hunt.

Deer are browsers, eating many different plants, fruits, nuts and grains depending on what's available. During harsh winters, mule deer will resort to eating bark and twigs to survive as they can also live in harsh regions. Both mule and white-tailed deer are delicious table fare, but the white-tailed deer takes the crown in taste, as it often dines on crops farmers grow such as soybeans and corn throughout much of its range. They more typically live in areas with more agriculture, also foraging on plants, grasses, acorns, beechnuts, hickory, pecans, fruit and more when in season.

Range & Habitat

Mule deer are known as a Western deer, the majestic monarch of the Rocky Mountains. Mule deer and its subspecies range from the deserts of northern Mexico all the way into southern Alaska. Western Nebraska is the mule deer's eastern border and the Pacific Ocean is its western border. They are not as numerous as the white-tailed deer, preferring the solitude of the high mountains or the openness of the prairie and desert.

The white-tailed deer is an edge dweller and has adapted well to farmlands across the country, where they come out from the forests to feed at night. Their range begins on the East Coast and sprawls west into Idaho, and from as far north as the Yukon south down into Mexico, Peru and Ecuador.

Firearms, Archery & Other Equipment

Firearms

To hunt deer, several different types of firearms can be used. Firearms that are effective for deer include the bolt-action rifle, lever-action rifle, single-shot, modern semiauto rifle and muzzleloader in a wide range of calibers; the muzzleloader is available in the traditional flintlock, percussion sidelock and modern in-line models. All of these styles can work well for hunting deer, so choose the gun that is best for

A broadside shot is the best position to shoot a deer, but be aware of any limbs and branches, which can change the course of your bullet or arrow.

An alert white-tailed deer may stomp and snort if she senses a threat in the area.

your specific needs. Keep in mind that not all of these firearms may be legal in your state for hunting deer, so check with your state's game laws before choosing one.

Shotguns and slugs (specialized big-game shotgun ammunition) can also be used for harvesting deer, as some states don't allow centerfire rifles due to safety concerns in increasingly populated areas. In recent years, high-quality, large-caliber pistols have also become more popular in the big-game hunting scene.

Depending on the type of habitat, shots at deer can be on the long side, 100 yards or more, so a good riflescope is a prudent choice to add to your gun. There are many brands and models of high-quality riflescopes available on the market, so buy the best you can afford. You owe it to the animal to make a clean, accurate shot. You don't have to spend a fortune – there are some fantastic mid-range priced scopes available.

Choosing the Right Caliber

Though a highly debated topic, a dead deer is a dead deer, and no amount of power behind your bullet will make up for lack of practice with a firearm. The best caliber is the one that you can shoot most accurately to quickly and humanely kill a deer. Here are some of the most widely used calibers today:

- .243 – The .243 is a cartridge that has light recoil and when using a quality bullet, it has enough weight to do the job. It is a great choice for youngsters and for shooters who are sensitive to recoil.
- .25 – .25-caliber rounds are good choices as they are slightly heavier bullets and can reach farther distances.
- .270 – Neck and neck with the .30-06 Springfield as one of the most popular deer rounds, the .270 allows the use of heavier bullet weights and is extremely accurate without too much recoil.
- .30 – The best all-around calibers are the .30s, with the .30-06 Springfield being the most popular. It has a wide range of bullet weights, allowing the one-rifle

The .243 Howa is an accurate and low-recoil gun, great for kids and adults who are sensitive to recoil.

shooter the chance to engage in almost all of North America's big game. Also, the .30-06 is widely carried by most retailers, making forgotten or lost ammo at the airport less of an issue.

- Handgun calibers – Choose .44 Magnum and above, such as the .454 Casull, the .460 and .500 Smith & Wesson. Deer have been taken with the .357 Magnum, but only under the best circumstances. Some handguns can also shoot rifle calibers very well.

Archery Gear

If you are new to bow hunting or would like to give it a try, we highly recommend that you go to an archery store and talk to a specialist. They will be able to help you find the correct bow and accessories that will fit your size, strength and skill level. Whether you'd like to shoot a compound bow or traditional recurve or longbow, you'll still need arrows with field tips for practice, broadheads for hunting and a target for practice. Getting set up with accessories like an arrow quiver, rest, sight, release or finger tab will depend on what type of bow you choose and how you want to shoot it. This is another area where the archery shop specialist can be a big help, as they'll be able to guide you in the right direction for the kind of hunting and shooting you'd like to do. Be sure to check your state's game laws regarding the minimum draw weight for hunting deer to make sure your bow qualifies.

Hunting

In the West, a popular technique to hunt mule deer is the spot-and-stalk method. To do this, find a vantage point of your hunting area on a high spot and carefully observe the area below for deer with a spotting scope or binoculars. When a deer is spotted, plan a route to stalk or sneak in closer to the deer without being discovered, taking into consideration the wind direction to hide your scent and noise. Only when

Deer Hunting Gear

- ☐ hunting licenses and permits
- ☐ camouflage and hunter orange clothing
- ☐ blind or treestand
- ☐ safety harness for treestand hunters
- ☐ scent control detergents, soaps and deodorizers
- ☐ binoculars and scopes
- ☐ cleaning tools, covered in cleaning section
- ☐ shooting stick
- ☐ rangefinder

An elevated blind helps a great deal to conceal your scent and movements when hunting deer.

you are close enough to make a good shot, set up and take it. Stalking mule deer is very difficult because they have incredible senses.

Hunting white-tailed deer can be much different. Their habitat can be huge tracts of forest or the broken wooded habitat in close proximity to farmlands. Try to spend some time before the season observing their movements as they move between their daytime bedding areas and nighttime feeding areas during the mornings and evenings. Unless disturbed, deer tend to follow many of the same paths. Once you've done your scouting, place yourself along these travel paths to intercept deer as they move. To counter the whitetail's keen senses, many hunters use a treestand to hunt from above, or hide themselves in a blind on the ground. Shots at white-tailed deer can be extremely close at only a few yards, or up to several hundred yards if out in the open. Use a shooting stick if you can to help steady your gun.

Tactics for archery are similar but in much closer proximities; most archery shots at deer occur at less than 35 yards, depending on the archer's skill. Due to this close proximity, great care must be taken to mask your scent and your movements. Specialized clothing, scent-reducing detergents, deodorants and soaps are all available to help minimize scent.

Whether hunting in the high mountains, desert, northern forests or near a local farm, deer hunting will test your skills and your patience. If you come home empty-handed, that's OK. Use your time in the woods to learn more about the deer's habits and to learn from your mistakes. When you finally do shoot one, your success will be that much more rewarding.

Shot Placement

Knowing when to shoot and not to shoot is an important part of being an ethical hunter. To drop a deer quickly, aim for its vitals, which is the lung and heart area located behind the shoulders. A broadside shot is the best scenario for gun and bow hunters. Quartering-away and quartering-toward shots are also alright for gun hunters, but archery hunters should only take quartering-away shots. The shoulder area covers too much of the vitals in a quartering-toward shot. And if the shot errs too far back, there's a

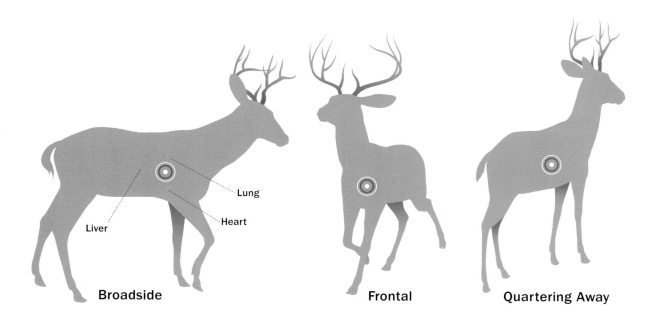

Broadside   Lung   Liver   Heart   **Frontal**   **Quartering Away**

greater chance of catching the gut area as the arrow or bullet travels through the deer at an angle. Shots from the rear should never be made by anyone, while head-on shots should only be reserved for more experienced hunters.

Field to Table

Venison is the filet mignon of wild game meats. It's an ideal protein – lean, yet tender, flavorful and juicy with endless possibilities in the kitchen. Handled and prepared correctly, venison should not be "tough" or "gamy," and cooking it should not be an intimidating task. The process to getting good venison, however, starts from the beginning – from making a good shot to proper field dressing, aging, packaging and finally cooking.

Field Dressing

A good dish at the table starts with proper handling in the field. Once on the ground, it is imperative to field dress and cool down the deer as soon as possible, especially if hunting in warmer weather. If left for too long, bacteria in the digestive system will start to spoil the meat. Depending on the weather, we recommend field dressing deer no later than one to two hours after it's been shot.

Before you begin, make sure the deer is dead before approaching it. Check for any reaction by carefully touching the eyes with a long stick or your gun barrel. Approaching a deer that is still alive may cause it to panic wildly and injure you. When you're sure it's dead, unload your gun or bow and move the deer to a more comfortable spot to field dress, if needed.

STEP 1. If desired, wear gloves and disinfect your knife. First, lay the deer on its back. Locate the anus on a buck and cut a circle around it; cut around the anus and vagina for a doe. The circle should be about 2 inches in diameter and your knife should be inserted about 4 inches deep, slightly angled outward to avoid cutting into the rectum. To prevent fecal matter from being expelled during the next steps, pull out a small section of the rectum and use a string or a zip tie to close the rectum shut.

Tools for Field Dressing & Butchering

- ☐ sharp knives (we use a combination of the Buck knife, Havalon and fillet knife)
- ☐ latex gloves (optional)
- ☐ disinfecting wipes, for wiping hands and knives
- ☐ clean rags
- ☐ rope or game cart to extract deer
- ☐ small pieces of string, twine or zip ties
- ☐ large zip-lock bag to save heart and liver
- ☐ flashlight
- ☐ trash bags
- ☐ cooler and ice
- ☐ Weston or FoodSaver vacuum sealer and packages
- ☐ Weston electric or manual meat grinder

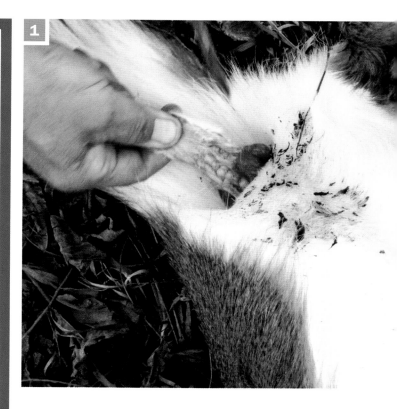

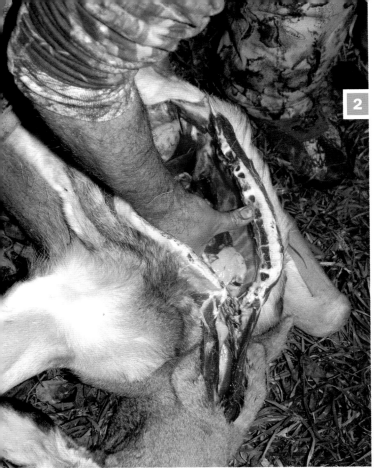

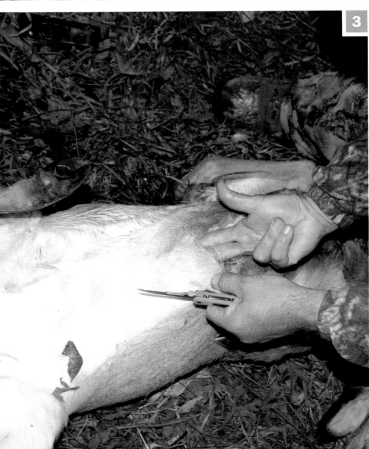

STEP 2. Locate the bottom of the sternum then cut upward through the sternum, with the blade edge turned up to prevent puncturing any organs. Cut far enough to be able to locate the trachea and esophagus. If possible, have another person hold the deer in place.

STEP 3. Now facing toward the anus, insert your index and middle finger under the initial cut to form a "V" with your fingers. Gently pull up the hide with your fingers to get your knife underneath, blade turned upwards between your fingers, and carefully cut through the abdominal wall, skin and fur. Cut all the way down to near the anus, being extra careful not to cut into any digestive organs, including the intestines and bladder. If the doe is lactating, do not cut through the udder, but cut around it and remove it. For a buck, cut around the penis and testicles, then reach into the body cavity to cut them off at their base. Disinfect your knife as necessary.

STEP 4. If desired, cut out the heart and liver and place in a zip-lock bag. Next, reach as far up the chest and neck as you can and cut through

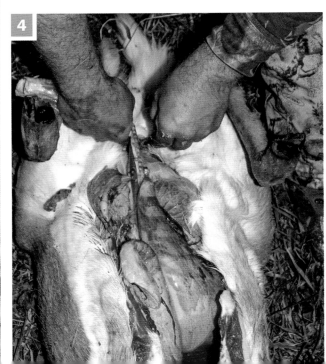

both the esophagus and trachea, then grab the loose ends and start pulling it out and toward the deer's hind end. The upper organs should come with it. Free the lower organs by separating the diaphragm from the ribs on both sides of the body cavity. Next, tip the deer over so the organs roll out. You may need your hands and knife to help the process. Lay the deer on its stomach for a few minutes to drain out blood, but do not allow the cavity to be contaminated with dirt or debris.

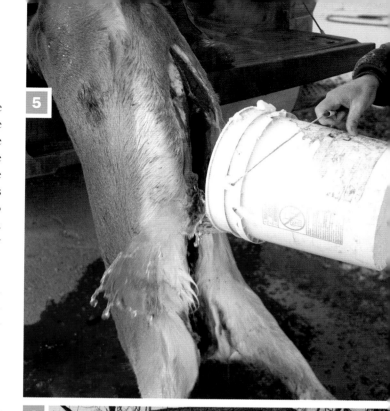

STEP 5. If the cavity has been tainted by contents from the intestinal or urinary tract, typical of a gut shot, wash out the cavity with snow or water. After you're done, dry out any excess water as soon as possible with rags. If the temperature is below 40 degrees Fahrenheit, allow the deer to cool down by propping the chest cavity open with a stick. If it's warmer than that, place several bags of ice inside the body cavity, but make sure to keep the chest cavity dry.

STEP 6. Age the deer by hanging it from a sturdy tree limb, a meat pole or inside a garage if the temperature is in the mid-30s. Many people hang deer by the hind legs, but we are used to hanging our deer by the neck — we started out hunting without owning a gambrel and that's how we've been hanging our deer since. Plus this allows any leftover blood to drain out. Professional butchers may say otherwise, but it has worked well for us so far and our venison has tasted perfect. If weather and temperature permits, leave deer hanging for at least three days (see sidebar on aging). If hanging inside a garage, place a small plastic pool or tarp underneath the deer to catch any draining blood.

STEP 7. Finally, remove the tenderloins, or inside straps, located underneath the spine. These inside loins are so tender that they do not need aging. Eat them for dinner that night or freeze for later use.

Aging Venison

If the outside temperature is between 32 and 40 degrees Fahrenheit, hang the gutted deer outside or in a cold garage for a few days to age. Aging allows the muscles to relax after rigor mortis, allowing them to become tender and develop a better flavor – the same idea behind aged beef. We like to age our deer in a garage for three to five days, depending on the weather and temperature conditions, but this may not be a possibility for some hunters due to location and time of year. If you find yourself in this situation, it is possible to age skinned and quartered deer by hanging meat in a spare refrigerator (at 35 degrees) or even in a cooler filled with ice. If using a cooler, lay the meat on a layer of ice and pour more ice on top of it. Be sure to have the meat in plastic bags or have a piece of plastic sheeting between the meat and ice to keep them from coming in direct contact, and not allowing the meat to become soaked with water. Keep the drain plug open and place the cooler in a shaded area on a downhill incline to allow the melted ice water to drain. Check throughout the day and add more ice as needed – do this for at least two days. Keep an eye out for flies so they don't contaminate the meat.

Although preferable, not being able to age venison is not the end of the world. We have eaten deer that were butchered immediately and it tasted just fine. You may run into this situation when temperatures are below freezing or really warm, and you don't have a spare refrigerator to use or the time to age meat in a cooler with ice. It is best to butcher the deer in those situations. Proper aging does not happen when meat freezes, and trying to thaw a whole deer is a mess.

Skinning & Breaking Down

Some people choose to send their deer to a processor, but we would rather save the hundred bucks. After all, if you're hunting to combat the rising prices of meat at the grocery store, why add to the cost of your venison? But if you're short on time and have to go through a processor, make that sure that you are getting your deer back and not someone else's; that person may not have properly cared for their deer in the field like you did, and that will affect the meat's taste.

STEP 1. Depending on where you are quartering your deer, have a cooler with ice on hand. With the deer hanging by the neck, locate the wrist joint below the shank on the front legs. Cut each around the joint to break the hide, then twist the joint to remove and discard the lower part of the legs.

STEP 2. Move down to the hind legs and locate the ankle joints. Cut around each joint to break the hide, then twist to remove. Do not cut through the scent glands located just above this joint. It looks like a bump or large tuft of fur. Cutting the glands will contaminate your knife and ruin any meat that it touches afterward.

STEP 3. Looking at the inside of the shoulders, cut a line from the end of the broken joint to the chest cavity on both sides. This will make the deer easier to skin later.

STEP 4. Cut the hide around the circumference of the neck by the base of the skull, with the blade turned out. Cutting from the inside out prevents your knife from getting dull too quickly, which will happen if you try to cut through fur. Then cut a line from the chest cavity to the first cut around the neck at the base of the skull. Grab the hide by the top of the neck and pull downward, using your knife to release stubborn areas.

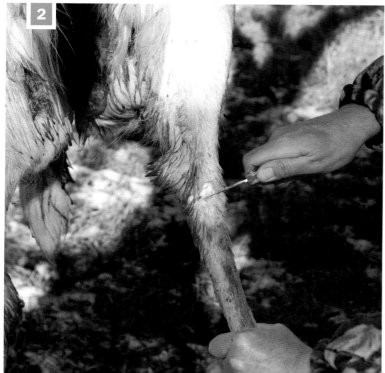

STEP 5. Continue to pull the hide away from the front legs and down the body. Once you get to the tail, cut through the tail (on the meat side) to continue removing the hide from the hind legs until the deer is completely skinned, except for the head.

STEP 6. Remove the shoulders. This will be easy because the shoulders are connected to the body by only muscle. Put the shoulders in a cooler with ice while you work on the rest of the deer.

STEP 7. Now remove the hindquarters by following the contours of the pelvis. Cut or twist off the ball joint that connects the femur to the pelvis.

STEP 8. Remove the loins. Follow the contour of the spine and the top of the rib cage with your knife, and pull away the loin as you cut. It should come off as one piece of very tender meat.

STEP 9. Remove meat from the neck by filleting it off on both sides. Trim off any leftover meat on the carcass. There will be a fair amount around the rib cage, and some hunters even trim out the rib cage. These trimmings are perfect for making venison burger and sausage. Discard the carcass according to your state's regulations.

Cleaning & Packaging

A sharp fillet knife is necessary for cleaning venison. Before packaging, trim as much fat as you can off the meat. Also, remove any stray hair and trim off the bruised meat from around arrow and bullet wounds. You can trim off the silver skin, but that can mostly wait until you're ready to cook.

Fast, powerful and easy to clean, the Weston Pro Series Meat Grinder is a workhorse in our kitchen.

The way you break down the quarters will depend on what you plan to do with it. If you plan on making sausage or burgers, simply debone the quarters and cube them for grinding; we have a Weston Pro Series Electric Meat Grinder and it's perfect for our needs. If you plan to make steaks and roasts, then separate the muscle groups at their seams to get different cuts. Bigger muscles in the hindquarters such as the bottom round and top round are wonderful for steaks — just remember to cut steaks across the grain. Smaller muscles like those on the shoulders can be kept together to get larger roasts for braising, or cubed for stew meat. We also like to keep the front shanks whole for braising.

If hunting is going to be a regular activity for you, invest in a good vacuum sealer. It is a very handy tool for meat hunters and will keep meat fresh in the freezer for up to three years. Each morsel of venison will taste just as good as the day you butchered it. We highly recommend vacuum sealers made by Weston and FoodSaver.

Cooking Venison

Venison is special, like any food that you may cook in the kitchen, with its own set of rules that need to be followed. We've met too many people who try to treat wild game like beef or chicken instead of taking the time to learn how to properly cook it. They'll ruin it and then blame the meat, then spread this false information to other people who have never even tried

Meat from the hindquarters can be cubed, marinated and grilled to make kebabs, like these apricot and curry venison kebabs.

it. Surprisingly, many hunters are guilty of this, too. The truth is, if you do everything right, venison should taste similar to lean, grass-fed beef.

Also remember that a deer's diet, sex and age can affect its taste. For example, a Nebraska white-tailed deer that lived on corn may taste quite a bit different from a Wyoming mule deer that lived on sage and shrubs. Young deer and does generally taste more tender and mild than older, rutting bucks, but not always.

Grilling & Pan Searing Venison

The only rule for grilling and pan searing venison is to not overcook it, and we reserve these cooking methods for less sinewy parts of

Adrenaline and Meat

It's important to make a good killing shot, especially if you're going to eat what you hunt. Nonfatal shots will allow a deer to run, causing adrenaline and lactic acid to build up in its system. This can change the taste, texture and smell of meat. When you know you have made a good shot, be patient. Do not let the deer see you and do not chase after it. Not all killing shots cause deer to drop in its tracks. It's normal for deer to run a ways, but they will eventually drop and bleed out quietly. If you immediately chase a wounded deer, the knowledge of your presence will cause the deer to panic and run.

the deer like the backstraps and steaks from the hindquarters. Other than that, we prepare our venison steaks the same way we would a medium-rare beefsteak.

Always remember to allow steaks to come to room temperature by taking the meat out of the refrigerator one hour prior to cooking. Remove all of the silver skin and fat from the steaks by slipping a sharp, pointy knife underneath; silver skin will contract and make your meat curl and tough when heated. Loins do not need any marinating and are best grilled whole over direct high heat – though, they are easier to pan sear if cut into smaller steaks. Steaks from the hindquarters can benefit from an acid-based marinade such as lemon juice or vinegar, although it is not absolutely necessary; hindquarter steaks from a young deer are almost as tender as the backstraps. We like to cube the meat from an older deer, then marinate and grill them as kebabs.

When you've got good steaks, salt and pepper are all they need. Then just grill them on oiled grates or pan sear them in some oil until medium-rare – but not past medium – over direct high heat on the grill or medium-high heat on the stove; cooking times will vary depending on the thickness of your steaks. If you're pan searing large pieces of loin or round steak from the hindquarters, it is best to finish the steak in an oven preheated to 375 degrees Fahrenheit, as described in the recipe on page 22, to avoid burning the outside and allowing the inside to come to temperature.

Avoid using a meat thermometer to check for doneness; you will lose juices that way. Instead, use the finger test. This great trick is done by touching your middle finger to your thumb, then feel the base of your thumb with your other index fin-

ger – this is what a perfect medium-rare steak should feel like. Touch your thumb to your index finger and that is rare. Touch your thumb to your ring finger and that is overdone.

Braising & Roasting Venison

Roasting is best for tender and less sinewy parts of the deer. There are recipes out there that describe roasting entire venison shoulders and legs, though the dry heat of an oven does not do any favors for the tough connective tissues. Sear venison on the stove before roasting to get a nice crust.

The best way to cook whole roasts, shoulders or shanks is to slowly braise them for three to four hours, allowing connective tissues time to break down and soften. Season the meat first, sear it on the stove to get a good crust on the outside, then bake it with a braising liquid in the oven at 300–350 degrees until tender. This is where a Dutch or French oven comes in handy.

Venison roast can be braised and slow-cooked to become fork tender.

Venison Round Steak
with Cognac-Sautéed Morel Mushrooms

Servings: 3-4
Prep Time: 1 hr
Cooking Time: 25 mins

1 whole venison round
from a deer's hindquarter

kosher salt and freshly cracked
pepper, to taste

3 tablespoons of butter

1 teaspoon of extra virgin olive oil

1 pound of morel mushrooms, halved,
quickly washed and drained

pinch of dried or fresh thyme

1 teaspoon of chopped fresh parsley

¼ cup of cognac or whiskey

2 shallots, thinly sliced

1. Preheat oven to 375 degrees. Rinse venison round under cold water and pat dry with paper towels. Remove any silver skin and fat, then sprinkle generously with salt and pepper. Allow the meat to come to room temperature.

2. Heat an ovenproof or cast iron skillet over medium-high heat and add one tablespoon of butter. Dab steak dry with paper towels again and sprinkle some more salt and pepper just before cooking. Then sear both sides of the steak until browned and crusted, about two minutes each side. Next, place the skillet in the preheated oven to finish cooking, about 12 minutes for medium-rare on a fairly large round. Cooking time will vary.

3. Meanwhile, heat another skillet over medium heat. Add one tablespoon of butter and one teaspoon of oil to the pan. Add shallots and cook until just turning brown, stirring often. Then add morel mushrooms and a pinch of salt. Cook until mushrooms give up most of their moisture. To avoid overcooking the mushrooms, remove them from the pan, allow the liquids to evaporate and then replace the mushrooms. Carefully pour cognac or whiskey into the pan and allow it to reduce until almost gone. Remove the mushrooms from heat then stir in the last tablespoon of butter, thyme and parsley. Add salt and pepper to taste.

4. Allow venison to rest for five minutes, tented with foil, before slicing across the grain. Serve with mushrooms on top.

Venison top
& bottom round,
found in the hindquarters, are tender cuts that can be grilled or pan seared.

Persian-Style Venison Shanks with Saffron

1. Preheat oven to 300 degrees. Rinse shanks under cold water and pat dry with paper towels. Remove the top, thick layer of silver skin, which holds the muscle groups together, but leave the rest of the silver skin on. Salt and pepper all sides well. Combine turmeric, cinnamon and cardamom, and rub all over the shanks.

2. Heat two tablespoons of oil in a French or Dutch oven over medium-high heat. Dust the seasoned shanks with flour and brown both sides, about three to five minutes each side. Remove the browned meat and set aside.

3. Add more oil to French or Dutch oven, if needed. Lower heat to medium and add sliced onion and a pinch of salt, then sauté until translucent for five to seven minutes. Add three tablespoons of tomato paste, and stir for about 15 seconds. Pour in chicken stock and scrape the bottom of the pan to deglaze. Return the venison shanks to the pot and pour in enough water to cover the shanks three-quarters of the way. Sprinkle in a pinch of saffron.

4. Cover and cook shanks in the preheated oven for three to four hours, or until tender. Flip shanks over every hour. Add water if the broth gets too low. The meat should fall away from the bones, and the gristle should be tender. Serve with basmati rice and garnish with fresh parsley.

Servings: 2-3
Prep Time: 5 mins
Cooking Time: 4 hrs

2 venison shanks
   from the front shoulders

2 tablespoons of olive oil, plus more

all-purpose flour for dusting

½ teaspoon of ground turmeric

½ teaspoon of ground cinnamon

¼ teaspoon of ground cardamom

pinch of saffron threads

3 tablespoons of tomato paste

1 large onion, sliced

1 can of low-sodium chicken broth

kosher salt, to taste

cracked pepper, to taste

freshly chopped parsley, for garnish

Venison shanks, located on the front legs, do not have to go into the sausage pile. They are perfectly delicious braised.

Wild boar can offer a dangerous, heart-pounding hunt.

CHAPTER 2

WILD HOG

Sus Scrofa, the wild pig or feral swine, is quite possibly the most prolific, fastest growing game in North America and many parts of the world – no other domestic animal can "turn wild" and reproduce faster than the pig. From a manageable population of 2 million in 1990 to an estimated 5-8 million in 2014, the population has quite literally exploded. In Texas alone, it is estimated that over 2 million pigs roam wild, and they are now believed to exist in almost all of the lower 48 states, Canada and Mexico. They are a major threat to habitat, other wildlife and agriculture. Voracious feeders, wild hogs are able to eat almost anything, destroying millions of dollars worth of cropland and habitat every year. In some areas, they are displacing native species.

What does this mean for you? It means that many states consider wild hogs pests and they want them gone, opening up hunting opportunities almost everywhere, and if not in your state then in a state nearby. If you have not yet stepped into big-game hunting, then wild hogs are the perfect animal to start with, being widely available and relatively cheaper than other big-game hunts. Depending on what kind of experience you're looking for, hog hunting can be a dangerous, heart-pounding game if you're aiming for a boar, a trophy hunt if you're looking for large tusks, or a fine tasting meal in a smaller, younger meat pig.

Hog History

Wild pigs, or all pigs, are not native to North America. They were originally brought here as domestic pigs by European explorers for food. Knowing that pigs are hardy animals and fast reproducers, those explorers also released them for future explorers to have a reliable food source at their disposal. As settlers colonized the new continent, they brought even more pigs with them for food and farming. As pigs escaped or were released, the seeds of an explosion were planted. In 1912, the first Eurasian wild boars were brought into the United States and released onto a preserve for hunting purposes in Hooper

Bald, N.C. Some of these Eurasian boars escaped and bred with feral pigs, producing a hybrid that is now found throughout North America. Some of the boars from this preserve were also transplanted to nine other states for hunting purposes.

Biology

The wild pig can grow to very large sizes, with some controversial behemoths reported at over 1,000 pounds. Most big boars will weigh around 250 to 300 pounds, with adult sows weighing in at around 150 pounds.

Pigs grow very quickly, reaching sexual maturity in as little as six months after birth. They can have litters of six to eight piglets or more, two to three times per year, allowing pigs to take over an area very quickly. Another reason for their population explosion is that they fear little threat from predators once they reach 40 pounds; wild pigs are built like tanks and are tough to take down. What's more, pigs also have an average life expectancy of about 8 years.

Wild pigs can be black, red, white, brown or different combinations of mottled spots. Piglets are born with stripes to help them stay camouflaged. Opportunistic feeders, wild pigs will eat almost anything. They can mow through a farmer's newly planted field in a single night or eat other animals both dead and alive, such as fawns, snakes, frogs and lizards. They have been seen gorging on the carcasses of dead cattle and will eat the eggs of ground-dwelling birds like turkey, pheasant and quail. This aggressive predation will often chase other wildlife away from the area.

Range & Habitat

Wild pigs are highly adaptable animals, able to live in hot climates as well as the snowy environs of the upper United States and into Canada. One requirement that they do have is living within a short distance of water. Due to their lack of sweat glands, pigs must find water to wallow in and cool off during warm weather. As the weather warms, pigs will often become nocturnal and only be seen in the early morn-

Wild pigs can build extensive trails and mazes as they bulldoze their way through brush.

Wild pigs have an average life expectancy of 8 years. When sneaking through bedding areas, you may find skulls from previous generations of pigs.

ings or late afternoons and evenings when the temperatures are tolerable.

Wild pigs have been reported in most states except Delaware, Rhode Island and Wyoming. Even Hawaii has a large population. Because of the heat and lack of water, pigs are not found in desert areas.

Although wild pigs can live in a variety of environments, they prefer areas with plenty of water to keep them cool and areas with heavy cover for bedding. Wild pigs thrive in the forested areas of the southern United States and north to Canada, and have taken a liking to California's fertile croplands and mild temperatures. They are very mobile animals and will travel far to find areas that meet their habitat, food and water needs.

With short and powerful compact bodies, wild pigs are capable of bulldozing tunnels through thick brush. In heavily trafficked areas, you will be surprised by the maze of these trails. Oftentimes, these brushy areas are near croplands where they can come out at night to feed.

Firearms & Ammunition

The wild pig is a tenacious animal, and it takes a tough bullet to bring one down quickly and humanely. A rifle caliber no smaller than a .223 combined with a well-built bullet should be used – anything smaller and you will have a hard time bringing down a full-grown pig.

A premium .223 bullet is adequate. A .30-caliber bullet like the .30-06 is probably the best, but other calibers such as the .270 and .280 get the job done just as well. The .30-30 is made for shooting in close quarters and the .45-70 is a good pig thumper, too. Larger calibers such as the .375 H&H can and have been used, but those are entering the realm of overkill.

AR rifles are becoming more popular in hunting today and bullet manufacturers have stepped up to introduce some very good, tough bullets that can be used for pig hunting. However, if you are not using one of these premium bullets, you will not get the performance that you need out of your AR rifle. Traditional pump-action, single-shot, bolt-action, semiauto and lever-action long rifles in any good deer-hunting caliber will also work just fine for pig hunting.

When shooting a pig, remember that they have a tough hide to penetrate as well as the thick gristle plate that boars have to protect themselves from the tusks of other boars while fighting. Wild hogs also have very tough bones and an anatomy that differs from most other animals, making the use of a high-quality bullet with reliable expansion, weight retention and penetration essential. We personally like to use a bullet that is on the heavy side for its caliber, such as the Nosler Partition, Barnes TSX or TTSX, Hornady's InterLock or GMX, Remington's Core-Lokt and Winchester's Razorback XT, just to name a few. Do your research before you go hunting.

Many hunters also hunt hogs with archery gear, usually at close distances. When hunting over feeders, hunters will often shoot from a treestand. We are not bow-hunting experts, so we highly recommend that you talk to more experienced hunters at your local archery club or an archery specialist at a nearby hunting store. They will make sure you have everything you need to take down your first pig.

As always, before you go out for any type of hunting, check with your state's game regulations.

Hunting

Pigs can be hunted in many different ways. Out West, the spot-and-stalk method is mostly used. During the early morning or late afternoon, hunters sit high above a canyon or above known travel routes and use binoculars or spotting scopes to look for pigs as they travel to and from their feeding areas. Once spotted, the hunter will try to intercept the pigs and set up for a shot. A lot of these scenarios involve long-distance shots, sometimes a couple of hundred

Hunting guide Justin White at Chain Ranch in Oklahoma recovers a wild hog after a successful hunt. Hogs are very tough animals and can be aggressive when wounded – so always use extreme caution when approaching recently downed game.

In spot-and-stalk hunting, close-quarter shots are not unusual when getting into dense brushy areas where pigs bed.

yards due to the wide-open spaces found in western pig habitat. But there's a lot of dense brushy areas too, which of course means close, fast action.

In other parts of the country, where there are more dense forests and brush, some people will set up feeders to attract pigs. That's because the spot-and-stalk method would be futile in these thick areas where you simply can't see very far, with the exception of meadows and farm fields. This style is not as much of a sure thing as one would think. Pigs can come to the feeders like clockwork – but not always. They quickly figure out the game.

Dogs can also be used for tracking pigs in their brushy, forested environments. With this method, dogs will chase and corner the pigs so the hunter can move in for a kill. It is often a chaotic scene with dogs running around barking and howling, and pigs furiously keeping the dogs away. Sometimes, a pistol is preferable for this close action. A few hunters have even upped the ante – instead of using a firearm, a knife or spear is used to finish off the pig. If you have the nerve for it and like the intense adrenaline rush, there are guides that can help you fulfill this end.

Shot Placement

The best shot on a broadside pig is in the shoulder area. Because a pig's vital organs, especially the heart, are located low in the body, aiming low is preferable. If the pig is quartering away or quartering towards you, aim for an area that will bring the bullet between the shoulders and its vitals. A headshot is possible, but only if you hit the brain. A headshot should only be taken if absolutely necessary – a bad shot will only injure the pig.

Field to Table

After you kill your hog, field dress it quickly and get it cooled down as soon as possible. For a good meat pig, shoot sows or smaller males. Large boars have hormones that can make their meat taste gamy. This rule also applies to other big game. An animal's sex and age strongly influences the quality of its meat.

Tools for Cleaning a Wild Hog

☐ latex gloves
☐ large bucket or tub to catch blood and guts underneath
☐ sharp fillet knife or boning knife
☐ butcher's saw
☐ gambrel
☐ cooler of ice

Cleaning

Cleaning a hog may seem intimidating, but it's not much different than cleaning a deer. We had the opportunity to hunt at the Chain Ranch in Oklahoma, and our field guide Justin White showed us how easy the process is.

STEP 1. Hang the pig head-side down. If necessary, wash off any excess blood or dirt on the pig, then place a large tub directly underneath it to catch blood and guts while you work.

STEP 2. Using a sharp knife, cut through the skin around the circumference of the hind legs, a few inches above the hooves. Do the same on the front legs.

STEP 3. Cut a "V" through the skin starting from the cuts you just made above the hind feet, ending at a point in the middle of the abdomen, or in front of the penis for a male. Cut another "V," now upside down, starting from the front legs so that the points of both "V's" are connecting. Be careful not to puncture through the meat or abdomen.

STEP 4. Carefully fillet the top "V" flap away from the body to expose the testicles. Flip the flap over so that it's hanging off the other side of the pig.

STEP 5. On a male, cut the tubes that extend from the testicles. Cut the testicles away from the body as far back as you can and flip them over to the other side of the pig.

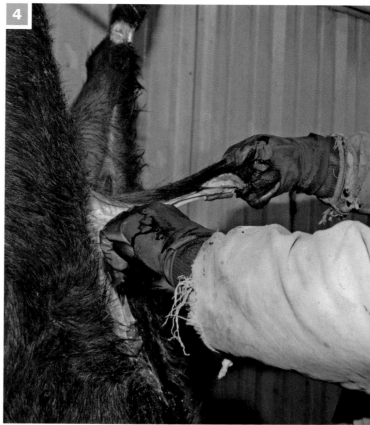

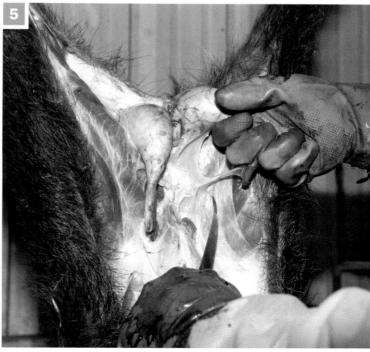

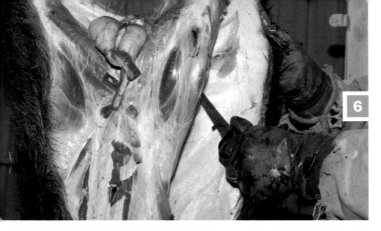

STEP 6. Start to separate the skin from the body by peeling it away from the meat and using your knife to help at difficult spots that won't give.

STEP 7. Cut through the tail to continue peeling back the skin. Continue peeling all the skin, including the skin on the front legs and the bottom "V," stopping when you get to the base of the head.

STEP 8. When you get to the head, use your saw to separate the head from the spine, which should bring all the skin with it. Use the tub to catch everything.

STEP 9. With a sharp, heavy knife, cut through the sternum and then through the belly flap all the way up to the pelvis to open up the body cavity, being careful not to puncture the stomach or intestines.

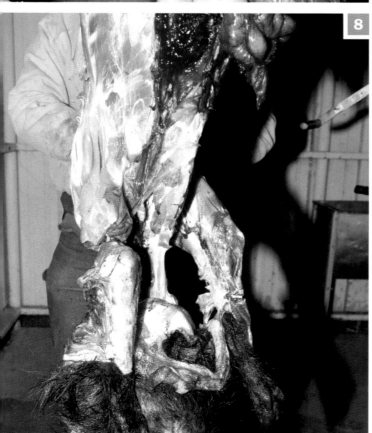

STEP 10. Pull the entrails out, including the heart and lungs, allowing the tub to catch it all. Use your knife to help release the organs from the diaphragm.

STEP 11. Cautiously remove the bladder. It sits in a hollow against the pelvis. Be careful not to puncture it.

STEP 12. Remove the inner tenderloins attached to the spine with a fillet knife.

STEP 13. Saw off the front hooves and discard. Then remove both front shoulders from the body. The shoulders are not attached by bone, so they will release easily by cutting the connective tissue.

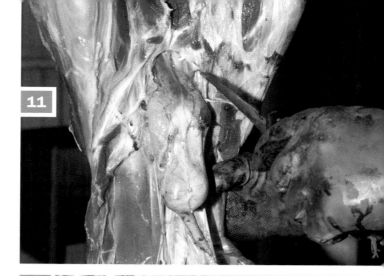

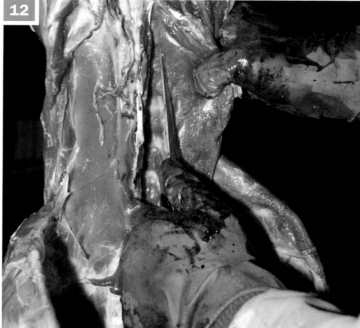

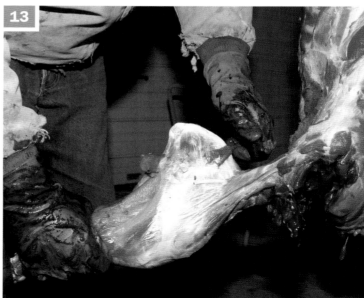

STEP 14. Turn the pig around and carve out the outside loins, which begin at the top of the pelvis.

STEP 15. With a saw, remove the ribs. Trim off any leftover meat on the body and save it for grinding. Then remove the spine by cutting where it connects to the pelvis. Save the bones for stock or discard.

STEP 16. Saw through the pelvis between both hams to separate.

STEP 17. Finally, saw the hooves off of the hindquarters.

Cooking Wild Boar

Meat from wild pigs and domestic pigs is different. Although they may taste similar, wild pigs have a much more active lifestyle, resulting in leaner meat. You won't get the nice big hams, shoulders and Boston butts so characteristic in farmed pigs. Unless you're equipped to scald an entire pig to keep the skin, which most hunters are not, you won't get much bacon either. Instead, we like to treat wild pigs much like deer. The loins will be tender, good for grilling and searing, while the shoulders and hams are best for braising and grinding. If your hog is big enough, you might get some nice ribs to marinate and put on the grill.

Although wild pork should be cooked thoroughly due to the risk of trichinosis, the same parasitic disease found in domesticated pigs, this doesn't mean that you should overcook it. The good news is that the United States Department of Agriculture (USDA) has recently lowered its safe cooking temperature for pork from 160 degrees Fahrenheit to 145 degrees, allowing pork to stay moist and remain slightly pink inside. If you're really worried, 150 degrees is a happy medium.

Braising & Roasting Wild Pork

The tougher parts of the pig like the shoulders and hams are best braised. You can choose to braise the leg whole or deboned, and then slowly cook it in a liquid at a low temperature. Assuming that your hams and shoulders won't have any skin and fat on them, it is important that you braise or roast wild boar covered, allowing steam to fall back on the meat to help keep it moist.

We don't recommend slow roasting skinless leg without liquid and uncovered. The combination of a dry oven and meat with no fat on it is not an ideal situation for wild game. By the time the leg is cooked through, the outside will be completely dry. If you're going to cook an entire leg, a slow braise is the way to go. If you want your meat slightly brown and crusty, remove the cover during the last half hour. These guidelines can help you modify your favorite pork recipes to work for wild boar.

Roasting the loins is a different story, and much easier. Season them with salt, pepper and other spices, then sear in a pan of butter over medium-high heat for two minutes per side to get a nice color. Finish the loins in a 400-degree oven, uncovered, for 10 to 20 minutes, or until 145-150 degrees internally. We recommend brining loins for four hours before roasting (see the Waterfowl chapter for a brine recipe).

Grilling Wild Boar

Grilling is best left to the loins. You can either rub the loin with your favorite spices or marinate before grilling. We highly recommend brining the loins for four hours, which has worked great for us to keep them moist, flavorful and juicy (see brining recipe in the Waterfowl chapter). Remember to take the meat out of the refrigerator an hour prior to grilling to allow for even cooking, then grill them just like you would domesticated pork. With a food thermometer, make sure the loin's internal temperature reaches at least 145 degrees to kill any parasites. Cooking time will vary depending on its size. When cooked, allow the loin to rest loosely tented in foil for at least five minutes.

Though tricky, wild boar ribs can also be grilled. To help tenderize the meat, we suggest marinating them overnight in a mixture that contains an acid such as vinegar or lemon juice. Then remove the ribs from the marinade and rub them with your favorite spices. Allow the ribs to rest at room temperature, covered, for an hour. Finally, grill them until cooked through, basting with reserve marinade or barbecue sauce. However, for foolproof tender wild boar ribs, we suggest braising them like in the following recipe.

Ecuadorian Roasted Wild Boar Leg

Servings: 20 (2 tacos each)
Prep Time: 3 days
(resting & marinating)
Cook Time: 6 hrs

10-pound whole wild boar leg
    (skinless)

juice of 2 limes

20 cloves of garlic, minced

1½ tablespoons of ground cumin

4 tablespoons of kosher salt

½ tablespoon of ground black pepper

1¼ cup of pork lard (manteca)

8 cups of inexpensive beer for marinating, plus 6 cups of beer for baking

2 tablespoons of achiote powder
    (ground annatto seeds)

8 yukon gold potatoes,
    cut in halves or thirds

Hornado de Chancho,
or roasted pork leg, is a classic dish in Ecuador.

1. Clean the leg as much as possible, making sure to remove any hair and blood clots. With a sharp knife, remove as much silver skin as you can.

2. In a bowl combine the minced garlic, ground cumin, salt and pepper. Squeeze lime juice all over the leg. Then make incisions all over the leg and stuff with the garlic mixture. Rub the rest of the mixture on the leg. Let the leg rest in the refrigerator, covered, for 24 hours.

3. After 24 hours, pour eight cups of beer over the leg. Cover and put the leg back in the refrigerator and let it marinate for 48 hours. Flip the leg over three to five times over the course of these two days.

4. Preheat oven to 400 degrees. Discard the beer marinade and place leg in a roasting pan. Generously rub more salt and one tablespoon of achiote powder over the leg and place dabs of lard over the top of the leg, about one-quarter cup. Bake it for 30 minutes at 400 degrees.

5. Meanwhile, melt one cup of lard in a saucepan and mix in the remaining tablespoon of achiote. Add six cups of beer and bring to a simmer. Lower the oven to 350 degrees. Take the leg out and bathe it with the beer and lard mixture. Then cover the pan with foil and return it to the oven. To keep the leg from drying out, you need to baste the leg like this every 30 minutes.

6. After three hours, flip the leg over, then lower the heat to 325 degrees and cook for two more hours, continuing to baste the leg with the pan juices every 30 minutes. Continue to keep the leg covered in the oven.

7. Add the potatoes to the pan and sprinkle a generous pinch of salt over them. Cover the pan again and cook for an additional hour, or until the potatoes are tender. Total cooking time should be six hours for a 10-pound leg.

8. Finally, shred or slice the meat. Serve with salsa, avocado slices, hominy, tortillas and rice.

Wild Boar Ribs
with Juniper

1. Preheat the oven to 225 degrees. Rinse the wild boar ribs under cold water, pat dry with paper towels and then place on a large piece of heavy-duty aluminum foil. Combine dry rub ingredients and pat a generous amount on both sides of ribs; note that this dry rub recipe makes several batches so do not use all of it. Fold foil into a packet and refrigerate ribs for at least one hour. If ribs are too large for foil use an oven bag.

2. Combine braising liquid ingredients in a microwaveable bowl and microwave for one minute. Place rib packet on a baking sheet and open up one end. Pour braising liquid into the packet, close it up again and tilt the packet back and forth to evenly distribute. Then bake ribs at 225 degrees for three hours.

3. Once tender, transfer braising liquid into a wide skillet. Turn heat to medium-high and reduce until it turns into a syrup consistency. Brush the glaze onto the ribs and broil until they are slightly caramelized – do not burn. Slice the ribs and toss with the remaining glaze or serve on the side.

Servings: 2
Prep Time: 1 hr & 10 mins
Cooking Time: 3 hrs & 30 mins

1 slab of wild boar ribs

Dry Rub
8 tablespoons of brown sugar

2 tablespoons of kosher salt

1 tablespoon of chili powder

½ teaspoon of cayenne pepper

½ teaspoon of dry mustard

½ teaspoon of onion powder

½ teaspoon of rubbed sage

½ teaspoon of Hungarian paprika

1 teaspoon of ground juniper

4 teaspoons of cracked black pepper

Braising Liquid
1 cup of white wine

2 tablespoons of white wine vinegar

2 tablespoons of Worcestershire sauce

1 tablespoon of honey

3 cloves of garlic, minced

To ensure tender and moist
wild boar ribs,
slowly braise them in the oven.

A brace of cottontails shot with a .22 Long Rifle.

CHAPTER 3

RABBIT

There are several species of rabbits in North America, the most common being the cottontail rabbit, jackrabbit and hare. In the western part of the United States, jackrabbits are often considered pests and are hunted as varmints or ignored altogether, so it is the cottontail and hare that we will look at closely. Generally considered better table fare than jackrabbits, cottontails and hares have light, lean meat comparable to the flavorful dark meat of chicken. Rabbit makes a great substitute for dishes that typically call for chicken, especially soups and stews.

Biology

The cottontail rabbit gets its name from its small white tail. It is mostly gray and brown in coloration on the sides and back, with white on its underside. Sometimes its color may best be described as rusty-brown.

The most common hare in North America is the snowshoe hare. It derives its name from its large, oversized hind feet, which it utilizes to effortlessly travel over the snowy reaches of its northern habitat. The bottoms of the feet are covered in fur to aid its ability to keep warm during cold, harsh winters. Hares stay camouflaged year-round by turning a rusty brown during the summer months and transforming into a ghostly white in the winter. Snowshoe hares can also be identified by the black tips of their ears, which are present throughout the year. Probably because of the cold regions in which snowshoe hares live, their ears are shorter than most other North American hares that have large ears to dissipate heat and keep them cool during hot weather.

Most rabbits and hares average three to four litters per year, and in good times that number can double. They can live up to nine or 10 years, but due to the nature of their existence as prey for many other species, few live past their first year.

Range & Habitat

Cottontails range over most of the United States, with the eastern cottontail thriving from southeastern Canada to the tips of Florida and Texas, and from the Atlantic coast westward through the prairie states to the foothills of the Rocky Mountains. The desert cottontail is found west of the Rockies from Montana south to New Mexico, and from Arizona west to California. As their name implies, the desert cottontail lives in the semi-arid grasslands of the West and are found at elevations up to 6,000 feet. Their bodies tend to be slightly smaller than their eastern cousins, but they make up for size with larger ears. Outside of the Rocky Mountain states and the extreme Northwest, cottontails can be found in most parts of the United States.

The snowshoe hare can be found in Alaska, Canada, New England and the Appalachian Mountains in Virginia. In the western United States they can be found from Washington south to northern California's high mountain ranges, as well as many northern states bordering Canada.

Cottontails and hares like forested and heavily brushed areas where they can hide and feel safe from the weather and predators. Downed trees and wood piles are excellent places for rabbits and hares to call home, preferably near areas of abundant food, along the edges of fields, pastures and open woods. They are often found near croplands, old abandoned farms where fields have gone fallow, or old orchards where fruit still falls for an easy meal.

If you're looking for a place to hunt, talk to neighbors, local farmers or biologists. Many landowners will likely allow you to hunt rabbits on their property, as they are becoming a less popular and under-utilized game animal.

Firearms & Ammunition

Hunting for rabbits and hares is typically done with shotguns and .22 rifles, but some hunters will bowhunt and trap for them too.

To limit damage to the meat, a scoped rifle is recommended, as a clean headshot is preferable. Whatever the type of rifle or manufacturer, make sure it is accurate, one that will allow you to consistently hit at an extremely small target. In recent years the .17 HMR has become a great rabbit gun with its ability to shoot very flat out to long distances.

Still, the .22 is the most preferred cartridge to use. Out of all the .22s, the .22 Long Rifle is the ideal choice. Its inexpensive price tag allows for plenty of target practice at the range and the chance to go out and hunt rabbits quite often. Its recoil is also very light, making it a favorite round to use for beginners and children. If you don't feel comfortable trying for the headshot,

In addition to .22 rifles, shotguns are a popular and suitable gun for hunting rabbits.

then a shot to the rabbit's front quarters can be effective; aim just behind the shoulder, much like you would do with a deer. Rifles – with open sights or scopes – have taken many of these tasty delights for generations. Many big-game hunters can recall starting out hunting rabbits and hares.

Shotguns can also be used, especially when your only chances are shooting at lightning-fast running targets. Rabbits can be one of the most challenging game animals to shoot. Their movements are quick and erratic, leaping and jumping in unpredictable patterns and angles instead of a straight line. They can run faster than 20 miles per hour and some hares over 35 miles per hour. Single shot, pump action, double barrel or semiauto – any shotgun will do, but a light and fast-handling gun will make a difficult task easier when tracking these super-quick targets. 12- and 20-gauge rounds are the most popular, but the venerable 28 gauge has a loyal following too. Use shot size 5 or 6, which is big enough to hit hard and small enough to pack plenty of pellets into a shotshell. Some hunters also use 7½, which will give even more pellets per round. A good choke to use is improved cylinder for close-range action, or modified for longer shots.

When hunting with a shotgun, keep in mind the possibility of getting pellets in prime parts of your rabbit or hare and the extra meat damage they might cause. So for cooking purposes, we prefer to use a .22 for rabbit hunting whenever possible.

Hunting

Rabbits and hares tend to be most active at dawn and dusk, so try to be ready as the gray of dawn approaches or as the sun is in its last couple of hours of daylight. Be sure to check your local game laws to make sure you are within the legal shooting hours.

Get out into the areas described earlier, places where thickets and brier patches are plenty and remember field edges too. As you approach these areas, slow down and be quiet. Rabbits are prey to many different predators which makes them extremely alert. Look well ahead, scan with binoculars if needed, and wait for a few minutes before moving forward as you may attract the unintended attention of any resident rabbits. If you do not spot any rabbits, move forward by taking several steps and then stop and look ahead. But be ready, when stopped you may unnerve a nearby rabbit that has been caught in the open, causing it to bolt. Also be aware out to your sides and directly behind you. Rabbits sometimes will freeze until you have passed and then try to make a quick escape. Even kicking small brush piles may chase out a rabbit from its hiding spot. Be erratic in your direction and pace. Don't be afraid to stay still for a minute or more. When that rabbit does run, make sure you give it a good lead when hunting with a shotgun. They are small and fast, only allowing the hunter fleeting moments to shoot before disappearing behind another bush. You must lead in front of the nose and follow through while pulling the trigger. An unfinished swing will inevita-

A cottontail rabbit comes out from its hiding place in the woods to feed in the late afternoon.

Rabbits and Tularemia

Also known as rabbit fever, deer fly fever, Ohara's fever or Francis disease, tularemia can be spread to humans by rabbits through the eyes, open cuts and wounds. In the United States, the majority of cases can be traced back to rabbits, mostly cottontails. Symptoms in humans vary, and if left untreated by antibiotics, tularemia can be fatal. The disease is believed to be more prevalent in rabbits during the summer and early fall months, when deer flies and ticks that carry and pass this disease to rabbits are more abundant.

We recommend that hunters use rubber gloves whenever possible while handling rabbits. An infected rabbit may show external ulcerations on infected areas where the animal was bitten by a tick or deer fly. Behavioral signs of the disease may include sluggishness, slow reactions and refusal to run. A more surefire way to identify a diseased rabbit is by checking for white or yellow spots on its liver, which is a common indication of tularemia. A healthy rabbit liver should be a solid red-brown color with no spots or discoloration. If you find otherwise, do not consume the rabbit. Even if your rabbit showed no visible signs of tularemia, it is a good safety precaution to cook rabbit meat thoroughly because heat is capable of killing this disease.

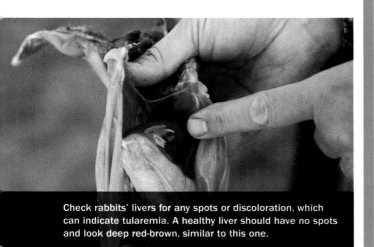

Check rabbits' livers for any spots or discoloration, which can indicate tularemia. A healthy liver should have no spots and look deep red-brown, similar to this one.

bly cause your shot to end up behind the rabbit.

During cold winter temperatures, a sunny day is often a good time to hunt because rabbits like to sun themselves on south-facing slopes. If snow is on the ground, look for tracks and see where they are feeding or where they are headed. This will give you clues as to what they are up to. Follow as quietly as possible, looking ahead for a rabbit that may stop to look back at what is trailing behind. Again, be quick with your aim and shot.

Hunting with dogs can also make for an exciting chase. Beagles are the perfect dog for this task as they have been bred to possess an acute sense of smell and a natural instinct to run a rabbit. An exposed rabbit has a tendency to run in a large circle when chased by a dog. A good tactic is to intercept the rabbit as it makes the round by placing yourself between where you think it will emerge and its home. Listen to your dog and as they approach, be prepared for some fast action. As always, know the location of the dog before shooting and never take a shot that is questionable. No rabbit is worth an iffy shot that could injure the dog, or worse.

Field to Table

Early-season rabbits are hunted in warm weather, making heat an important consideration when taking care of your game. To prevent rabbits from spoiling, do not leave them in the sun for long periods of time, whether they're in your game bag or in your vehicle. Try to field dress your rabbits within two hours after shooting them. Wear latex gloves whenever possible, as it is well known that rabbits can carry tularemia, a bacterial disease that can send you to the hospital. This is more apparent in hot weather. It is generally believed that harvesting rabbits after the first killing frost is preferable.

Keep your game away from flies, dirt and of course, like any game, get it cooled down as quickly as possible. Do not let the rabbit get wet, which can promote the growth of bacteria.

Cleaning

STEP 1. Loosen the rabbit's (or hare's) skin from its body by gently pulling and massaging the fur around its midsection.

STEP 2. Pinch the skin anywhere around the rabbit's midsection to lift it from the meat underneath and cut through. Continue to cut the fur around the circumference of the rabbit's body, being careful not to cut into any meat.

STEP 3. Next, pull and peel the hind section of the rabbit's skin over its hind legs to remove it, cutting through the tailbone. Then peel the front-end section of fur to the base of the rabbit's head. Pull its legs out of the fur. Snip off the paws.

STEP 4. Cut off and discard the rabbit's head to separate the fur from the front end.

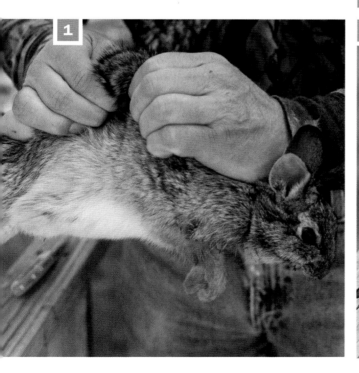

STEP 5. Lay the rabbit backside down on a flat surface and cut through the pubic bone by the anus. This will help detach the rectum when gutting.

STEP 6. Lay the rabbit on a flat surface and turn it so that its abdomen is up and its hind legs are closest to you. With a sharp knife, blade turned upward, cut through the rabbit's sternum, all the way up to its neck. Then turn the rabbit the other way and carefully continue the previous cut in the opposite direction all the way down to the anus, being careful not to puncture its intestines.

STEP 7. Pull out all of the inner organs from the rabbit, peeling from the trachea (windpipe) and detaching the rectum at the anus, and discard.

STEP 8. Lastly, rinse and trim the rabbit as necessary to remove any broken bones, dirt, blood, bruises or intestinal content.

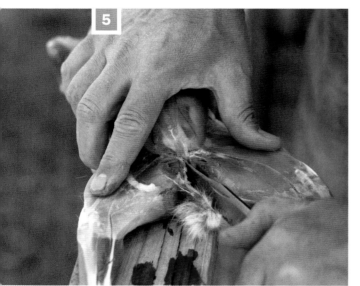

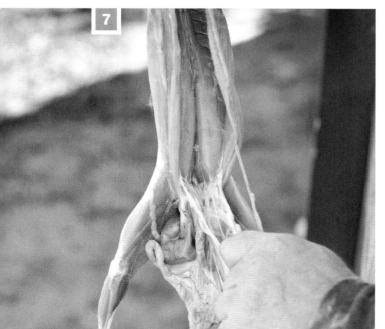

Breaking Down a Rabbit

See Chapter 4 for breaking down a squirrel.

Cooking Rabbit

Due to its light meat, rabbit will go well with all sorts of spices and flavors, much like chicken. We love to use rabbit for soups and stews, but it is also very tasty fried and grilled. Because rabbit is prepared without any protective skin to keep it moist, keep in mind that it can dry out easily. Unlike meats such as venison or beef that can be eaten at a juicy medium-rare, rabbit must be cooked thoroughly due to the possibility of tularemia.

Frying Rabbit

After you have broken down the rabbit (see Chapter 4 for breaking down squirrel), soak the pieces in buttermilk for 24 hours, or at least overnight. The acid in the buttermilk will help tenderize wild rabbit and keep the meat moist while cooking. Next, season and dredge the rabbit pieces like you would for fried chicken, and fry for approximately five minutes on each side. The recipe on page 48 is one of our favorites.

Roasting Rabbit

Roasting rabbit will require the help of a sauce or liquid to keep it moist, such as wine or stock. First cut the rabbit into pieces and season it with whatever spices you like. Allow the rabbit to absorb these spices by letting the rabbit sit at room temperature for at least an hour, covered. Then brown the rabbit in oil or butter in an ovenproof skillet, until both sides are golden. This added step of browning the rabbit imparts a flavor that you won't get in the oven, and this rule applies to any other roasted meats, whether wild or domestic. Next, add in whatever other herbs and spices you like to the pan, and then pour in a splash of wine or stock. Cover and cook the rabbit in a 400-degree Fahrenheit oven for 10-15 minutes, until it is cooked through but still tender. Do not overcook rabbit.

Grilling Rabbit

Since rabbit can dry out so easily, we don't often like to grill it, although it is possible. A few good rules to keep in mind are to marinate or brine the rabbit beforehand, which will help tenderize the meat and keep it moist on the grill. Bring the meat to room temperature by taking it out of the refrigerator one hour prior to grilling to allow for more even cooking; cold meat on the grill equals burned exteriors and raw, cold interiors. Wrapping with bacon is also a good trick to help keep it moist on the grill. Basting it with sauce or marinade will also help. Grill the rabbit until just cooked through.

Stewing & Braising Rabbit

Stewing and braising is where rabbit shines, and is just perfect for large, old rabbits that can be tough. If the rabbit is small, which is often the case for most wild cottontails, a soup or stew is where you'll be able to stretch that meat a little further; plus rabbit bones make great stock.

There is more than one way to stew a rabbit, but the basic method is the same: keep the rabbit moist, then cook it low and slow. As mentioned before, rabbit is a great alternative to chicken. The next time you're thinking about making chicken noodle soup, chicken potpie or even chicken and sausage gumbo, mix things up a bit and try rabbit instead.

Buttermilk Fried Rabbit

Servings: 2
Prep Time: 24 hrs
Cooking Time: 20 mins

2 large rabbits,
  cleaned and quartered

4 cups buttermilk, plus 2 tablespoons

2 cups of all-purpose flour

1 tablespoon of season salt

½ teaspoon of Hungarian paprika
  (or regular)

½ teaspoon of ground black pepper

½ teaspoon of dried thyme

½ teaspoon of cayenne pepper,
  or to taste

2 tablespoons of milk

vegetable oil

1. Remove as much silver skin as you can from the rabbit's legs and loins. The silver skin is the white film that clings to the top of the meat and will make the meat tough if it's not removed. Place rabbit pieces in a bowl and cover with four cups of buttermilk, or enough so that the meat is submerged. Cover and refrigerate for 24 hours, or at least overnight.

2. Take the rabbit meat out of the refrigerator to allow it to warm to room temperature for more even cooking. In a large bowl combine flour, season salt, paprika, black pepper, thyme and cayenne. Combine two tablespoons of milk and two tablespoons of buttermilk and add it to the flour. Stir with a fork so that the flour gets lumpy.

3. Heat about 1½ inches of oil to 365 degrees. Take the rabbit pieces out of the buttermilk and lightly salt them. Dredge them in the flour mixture, using your fingers to help press the flour onto the meat. Then fry in batches for five minutes on each side, depending on the size of the pieces. Check for doneness before serving.

Rabbit can be fried
just like chicken, soaked in buttermilk and dredged in your choice of seasonings and flour.

Coney Coddle

1. To make rabbit stock, place the rabbit pieces in a medium to large Dutch oven. Add water, celery, carrot, half an onion, ½ teaspoon of kosher salt, whole black peppers and bay leaves. Bring to a low boil, then cover and simmer for 30 minutes, or until rabbit is tender enough to shred. Skim off and discard any foam that forms on the surface of the broth.

2. After 30 minutes remove the rabbit from the Dutch oven and pick off as much meat as you can. Then set the meat aside. Return the bones to the Dutch oven and simmer for another 45 minutes, covered. Then, strain out the broth into another container, discard any solids and set aside.

3. Cook the bacon in a skillet. Drain off the bacon grease, but leave one tablespoon behind. Then cook the sausages in the same skillet until browned on all sides. Remove the sausages, then cook one sliced onion in the bacon grease for seven minutes or until translucent, stirring occasionally.

4. Layer a lidded casserole dish or the same Dutch oven like so: onion, bacon, sausages, leek, rabbit, thyme and garlic, seasoning each layer with plenty of cracked black pepper.

5. Finish off with a layer of potatoes, seasoning with a little more black pepper on top. Finally, pour in the rabbit stock. Cover tightly and bake at 300 degrees for 45 minutes, or until the potatoes are tender. Adjust your seasonings and serve with bread, or Irish soda bread if you'd like.

Servings: 6
Prep Time: 20 mins
Cooking Time: 2 hrs

- 2 wild rabbits, or 1 large domesticated rabbit, cleaned and cut up
- 5 cups of water
- 3 celery sticks, cut into thirds
- 1 carrot, chopped
- ½ an onion, halved
- ½ teaspoon of kosher salt
- freshly cracked black pepper, to taste
- ½ teaspoon of whole black pepper
- 2 bay leaves
- 1 large leek, white and some green parts sliced and wash thoroughly
- 2 sprigs of thyme
- 4 slices of bacon
- 1 onion, sliced
- 3 sausages, halved lengthwise and then halved again across
- 1 pound of mini Yukon Gold potatoes, halved
- 4 cloves of garlic, smashed

An Irish-inspired recipe,

this coddle is made of tender rabbit, sausage, Yukon Gold potatoes, bacon, leeks and herbs all in a savory rabbit stock.

A Nebraska fox squirrel staring down from a tree at its pursuers.

CHAPTER 4

SQUIRREL

As deer became more abundant, we left squirrel hunting by the wayside and hunted deer almost exclusively. But as of late, American hunters are remembering how fun and practical squirrel hunting can be, and are realizing how good squirrel can taste when prepared correctly.

There are several subspecies of squirrels in North America and we will look at the two most often hunted, the eastern gray squirrel and the eastern fox squirrel. Abundant small-game animals, they are found throughout North America and offer widely available hunting opportunities for both first-time and experienced sportsmen. What's more, squirrel hunting is relatively inexpensive compared to other game animals and requires minimal gear. As small targets, they can also provide great shooting practice for those interested in taking their hunting skills to the next level. The humble squirrel is the ideal quarry to teach beginners before they graduate to becoming effective big-game hunters.

Biology

While both the gray and the fox squirrels' habits are much alike, fox squirrels can grow a tad larger than the gray. However, squirrels rarely reach their full potential in growth, as they are a popular source of food for a wide variety of predators such as hawks, weasels, bobcats, snakes, coyotes and more. Some squirrels have lived upwards of 15 years in captivity, but in the wild a squirrel will live a much shorter life.

The colors of the gray squirrel are solid gray with hints of brown and a white underbelly, while the fox squirrel is mostly reddish-brown with a hint of gray on its back and an orange-red underbelly. Both subspecies also show an

all-black (melanistic) tendency in certain areas. These individuals have a dark pigmentation in their skin due to a mutant pigment gene, which can actually aid in concealment in dense forests.

Squirrels usually produce two litters of young per year and will mate around January and again in June. These dates vary between the lower and upper latitudes of their range. A litter may consist of three young on average, but can vary due to food and other environmental conditions.

As squirrels find safety in trees, they naturally nest there, too. If available, squirrels prefer a den or hollow, but they seem to do just fine in nests. Their nest, or drey, is mostly made of twigs and leaves. These nests are built in the forks of

Look for squirrel nests, or dreys, when locating hunting spots.

trees and are well camouflaged in the spring and summer, but when leaves begin to fall in the autumn they become highly visible. Look high when you are trying to spot one as they're never built low to the ground.

Range & Habitat

Gray and fox squirrels inhabit most of North America. Their range extends from New Brunswick west to British Columbia, then south into California and east to southern Florida. They have been transplanted into many of these areas and have thrived. Squirrels avoid the desert areas of the Southwest, but they are abundant in the high forest ranges of Arizona and New Mexico. They prefer hardwood forests to conifer types because of the nuts produced by hardwoods, but they will also inhabit pine forests and feed

on pinecones; favored hardwoods include oak, hickory, beechnut, pecan, walnut, black walnut and others. Squirrels also like to spend time around Osage trees.

Squirrels prefer to live in the canopy layer above the forest floor. They also prefer mature trees with an open understory, free from too much forest floor vegetation. This makes them feel safer from predators as they spend a good portion of their day on the ground searching for food and finding places to hide it. Squirrels love to hoard food and because they occasionally forget a few hiding spots, they have unwittingly become a mover of seeds, helping some trees and plants expand beyond their normal ranges.

Forests that have not experienced periodic burns or logging to clear out dense brush are not ideal habitat for squirrels. Trees near farmland are typically great locations because of the availability of food all year round.

Fox squirrels normally desire larger acreages of forest, but the gray squirrel is often content with calling a smaller area home. This would explain why they are often seen at local city parks, neighborhoods and in backyards raiding bird-feeders.

Firearms & Ammunition

Firearms used for hunting squirrels are usually shotguns or the trusty .22 rimfire. Shotguns are a good choice for hunting early in the season because trees will most likely be dense with leaves, making hunting difficult with a .22 caliber. But once the leaves begin to fall, the .22 Long Rifle (LR) is hard to beat.

Most squirrel hunters use rifles, but using pistols is a growing trend. Either way, make sure that your gun is accurate, and that goes for the hunter, too. The most accurate gun is useless unless the shooter puts in the time to practice and fine-tune shot groups into a target the size of a golf ball, which is about the size of a squirrel's head and the ideal place to aim on the animal in order to avoid damaging body meat. Whether you shoot a single-shot, bolt-action or semiautomatic rifle, make sure you practice and practice often. Accurate iron-sight shooting is an admirable skill, but for the most precise and humane dispatching of any animal, utilizing a scope is highly recommended, especially for beginners.

Comparatively speaking, .22 LR ammunition is not expensive when compared to centerfire cartridges. The same can be said for .17-caliber rimfires, which are high-velocity, flat-shooting rounds that are finding their way into the hands of more and more hunters.

A shotgun comes in handy when trees still have their leaves, which can make it almost impossible to catch a glimpse of a squirrel long enough to shoot it with a .22. You might hear them bark and chirp up above you, and see tails popping up here and there behind thick foliage,

The .22 Long Rifle is the perfect gun for shooting squirrels during the late season after the leaves have fallen.

but for the most part squirrels are difficult to spot during the early season. Shotguns will do the trick, allowing you to stalk close and spray pellets that will hopefully hit and drop one. Shotguns can also be safer to use than .22s, their stray pellets traveling nowhere near as far as a .22 bullet shot up into tree branches without a backstop – a .22 bullet can travel up to 1½ miles.

As for the correct shotgun gauge, anything from a 12 gauge all the way down to a .410 will do the job. Many hunters started out hunting squirrels with grandpa's old break-action .410

Once you spot a squirrel, stop and squat down or lean against a tree if possible. Move slowly and wait patiently for a shot.

single shot, but of course, the larger the shell, the more pellets available to hit your target. First, check with state laws for legal shot size, which can vary from state to state. Usually a midsize number 4, 5 or 6 shot will work, and in states where it's legal, shot size as large as 2 is acceptable. Keep in mind that a larger shot size will give you fewer pellets to hit your target, while a smaller shot size may spray too many small pellets into the meat.

Before you head out hunting, think about the most likely distances you will be shooting and choose your choke accordingly. If you are expecting close-range shots, use an improved cylinder. A little farther away? Go with a modified. Some people like the farther shots with a full choke, aiming at the squirrel's head for minimal damage to the body. As you can tell, the same firearms used for rabbits are also perfect for squirrels.

Hunting

Squirrels have excellent hearing and eyesight. They are social animals and communicate with each other frequently. Sneaking into the woods without being noticed is practically impossible, but learning to sneak in and use the squirrel's curious nature to your advantage is key. Cam-

Use a tree trunk or limb to steady your rifle for a clean shot.

A Quick Note on Shooting

When raising your gun to aim, move slowly because you don't want your movements to cause alarm. If possible, use a tree trunk or limb to steady your gun – remember that your target, the squirrel's head, is only the size of a golf ball. Then take careful and steady aim. When hunting with a rifle, always remember to make sure there's a solid backstop like a tree trunk behind the squirrel to stop the bullet.

ouflage clothing is not required when hunting squirrels but it helps to wear drab colors that blend in with the forest like browns and greens. If you have camo and feel more comfortable using it, go for it. Check with state laws regarding hunter orange, it is never a bad idea for safety's sake.

Still-hunting may be the most popular way of hunting squirrels – but it takes quite a bit of patience. When scouting the woods or entering for the first time, seek out oak or nut trees. These are some of their favorite foods. Also, look for their nests. Do not walk at an even, steady pace like you would normally; most animals know that sound differs between two-legged and four-legged creatures. The sound of your normal pace is unnatural and will quickly stand out in the forest. Instead, take two or three steps and then stop. Then take two or three more steps after the last pause. Walk in different directions as you cruise the forest, never moving in a direct line. Use your eyes to look for squirrels or nests, and also keep an eye out for signs of squirrel activity like empty nutshells under a tree.

Always listen for activity in the woods. Squirrels are noisy animals, whether they are moving from tree to tree, or chasing one another as they often do. Their chewing on the hard shells of nuts makes a fair amount of noise, as well as empty hulls falling to the ground. Running along the leaf-covered forest floor, they make a noisy go at it, fooling many a deer hunter whose hopes ran high expecting to see a deer – only to find that it was a squirrel. Pay attention to the sounds you hear and try to blend in. Listen intently and always look ahead to scan for activity.

Once the squirrels discover you are there, all activity will stop. They will immediately put the tree between you and themselves. If that should happen, stop. Squat down or lean against a tree and remain still. You might have to wait as long as 10 minutes, maybe more. Be patient – their curiosity will give them away sooner or later. After a reasonable amount of silence, they will reappear to look around the tree to check if all is safe and resume their activities, which should give you an opportunity for a shot.

It's also a good idea to wait a little longer for the possibility that other squirrels may emerge. If you take your first shot and are successful, don't run up and claim your prize immediately. Instead, remember where that squirrel fell to the ground and wait for activity in the woods to resume. You may soon claim a second prize.

Hunting with Dogs

Some hunters pursue squirrels with a dog and an entire book could be written on this subject alone. Some breeds are better than others – curs, walkers and Jack Russell Terriers to name a few – but what you need is a dog capable of running a squirrel up a tree. It must know basic commands such as "sit," "come" and the all-important "no." Once the dog has treed a squirrel and the shot has been taken, the dog will then retrieve the squirrel to its master.

As with hunting any game with dogs, it's always exciting and fun to watch a dog work with the handler. When instinct meets good training, that work turns into art.

Field to Table

As with other game animals, do not leave your squirrels in a hot, wet place, which promotes the growth of bacteria. Do your best to store your game in a cool, dry place, and clean them as soon as you get the chance. Squirrels tend to be more difficult to skin than rabbits due to their thick, tough skin that does not give so easily. There are many hunters who don't like to shoot squirrels simply because they don't like to clean them. But follow our steps and you'll be a squirrel-cleaning expert in no time.

Cleaning

STEP 1. Turn the squirrel upside down and lay its tail on a counter, the tailgate of your truck, tree stump, etc., so that the underside of its tail is facing up. With a strong, sharp knife, cut through the base of the tail, being careful not to cut through the skin on the other side. Next, slice a few inches of the skin on both sides of the tail and down its back, then use your fingers to separate the skin from the meat. This will help get the skin ready for pulling in the next step.

STEP 2. Lay the squirrel on the floor. Step on the tail and hold the squirrel's back legs with your hands. Using your foot as an anchor, pull the squirrel's legs upward to peel the skin down to the base of its head. Continue to hold onto the legs with one hand and use your other hand to pull the front legs free out of the skin. Stop at the base of the paws.

STEP 3. Continue to use your foot to hold the tail, peel the skin off its hind legs, stopping at the base of the paws.

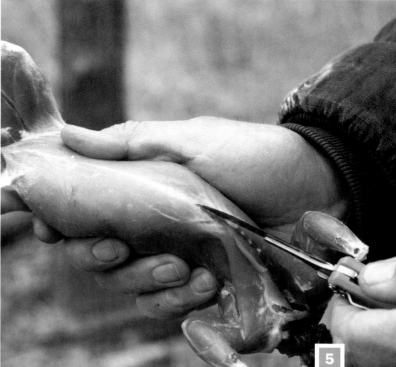

STEP 4. Next, cut the front legs from the paws by cutting away from you. Then separate the body from the head. Discard the head and skin. Cut the paws off the hind legs. If the squirrel is male, trim off its testicles and penis.

STEP 5. Hold the now skinless squirrel abdomen side up in one hand, its hind legs towards you. With a sharp knife, blade turned up, cut through its sternum all the way to the neck. Then turn the squirrel around so that its front legs are closest to you and cut through the skin down the abdomen from the base of the sternum to the anus, being careful not to puncture any intestines.

STEP 6. Using two fingers, pull the entrails out starting from the windpipe and separating at the rectum, then discard. Rinse the squirrel under cold water and pat dry. Freeze it in vacuum-sealed bags if you're not going to use it soon.

Cooking Squirrel

Squirrels taste like a cross between a lean white meat such as chicken or rabbit, and a more flavorful dark meat like dove. They are a viable, practical food source, being abundant and widely available in many parts of the United States. They can be braised, fried, grilled and roasted. Cooking methods and recipes between squirrels and rabbits are often interchangeable. For more information, see Chapter 3 under rabbit cooking tips.

Breaking Down a Squirrel

To break down a squirrel, you will need a fillet knife and a heavier knife to cut through joints. Because rabbits and squirrels are similarly built, these instructions will work for rabbits, too. To separate the front legs, feel for the shoulder blade and cut behind it. Rabbits' and squirrels' front legs are not connected to their bodies with bone – they are only attached and held together by muscle. Next, separate the hind legs. Cut where the thigh meets the body until you hit bone. Then give the leg a twist and you will feel a slight crack or pop, indicating the hip joint where the thigh and pelvis connect. Separate the legs by cutting through this joint. Next, you can choose to keep the back whole or cut it in two. We prefer to cut the spine between where the ribs end and where the inside straps start. Finally, remove as much silver skin as you can without sacrificing too much meat. Silver skin contracts when cooked and creates the illusion that the meat is tougher than it really is. This is the key to cooking tender squirrel.

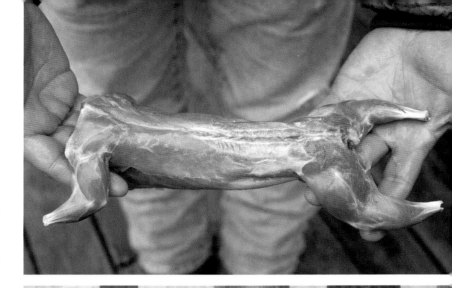

TOP: Squirrel is somewhere between light and dark meat. BOTTOM: A squirrel broken down into sections.

Braised Squirrel
with Salsa Verde

Servings: 2
Prep Time: 30 mins
Cooking Time: 5 hrs & 30 mins

2 squirrels, broken down

2 tablespoons of butter

kosher salt and
    freshly cracked pepper

1 cup of chicken broth

queso fresco cheese

1 large avocado, sliced

Tomatillo Salsa Verde

8 medium tomatillos,
    husked and rinsed

1-2 jalapeno peppers, stem removed

4 large garlic cloves, peeled

12 sprigs of fresh cilantro,
    roughly chopped

quarter of an onion, chopped

½ cup of water

1 teaspoon of kosher salt

Cilantro-Lime Rice

1 cup of uncooked long grain rice,
    rinsed

2 cups of water

1 tablespoon of olive oil

zest of 1 lime

½ teaspoon of kosher salt

3 tablespoons of chopped cilantro

1. Place tomatillos, jalapeno and garlic in a rimmed baking pan. Roast them below a hot broiler until jalapeno is roasted, garlic is browned and tomatillos turn a blotchy black. Garlic will brown faster – take it out before it burns. Allow ingredients to cool, then combine tomatillos (and their juices), garlic, jalapeno, salt, cilantro and quarter cup of water in a blender. Pulse until smooth. Pour into a bowl, mix in chopped onion and set aside.

2. Dab squirrel pieces dry with paper towels and season with salt and pepper. Melt butter in a skillet over medium-high heat and brown both sides. You don't have to cook the meat through.

3. Move browned pieces of squirrel into a slow cooker. Pour in the chicken broth and three-quarters of the salsa verde, reserving the rest to serve on the side. Cook on low for five hours, or until the squirrel is tender. Pour in more chicken broth if the liquid gets low. Serve with cilantro-lime rice, crumbled queso fresco cheese and fresh avocado slices.

4. To make cilantro-lime rice, combine rice, water, oil and salt in a small, heavy pot. Boil on high uncovered until the water reduces down to skim the top of the rice. Reduce heat to low and cook covered for about 15 minutes. Then take off the heat and keep covered for an additional five minutes. Finally, toss in cilantro and lime zest.

Squirrels slow-cooked
in salsa verde and served with cilantro-lime rice, sliced avocados and crumbly queso fresco cheese.

Grilled "Jerk" Squirrel

1. Combine marinade ingredients in a food processor. Pulse until smooth and spoon out some sauce into a small container, about ¼ cup, for dipping later. Pour the rest of the marinade in a zip-lock bag and add the squirrel pieces. Massage the bag to evenly distribute marinade and refrigerate for at least four hours, or overnight.

2. Prepare the grill then cook squirrels over direct heat, about five minutes each side or until cooked through. Do not overcook – this will dry out the meat and make it tough. Eat with your hands and serve with cold beer.

Servings: 2
Prep Time: 4 hrs & 30 mins
Cooking Time: 10 mins

2 squirrels, broken down

Marinade

4 tablespoons of vegetable oil

juice of 2 limes

2 tablespoons of white wine vinegar

4 scallions, chopped

1 tablespoon of ground allspice

1 serrano chili pepper, roughly chopped

3 cloves of garlic

1 tablespoon of fresh peeled ginger, roughly chopped

2 tablespoons of brown sugar

½ teaspoon of dried thyme

¼ teaspoon of cinnamon

1 teaspoon of kosher salt

The secret to tender, grilled squirrel is removing the silver skin and a good marinade.

The 12-gauge shotgun is the most widely used firearm to shoot wild turkeys.

CHAPTER 5

WILD TURKEY

The wild turkey is a native bird to North America. It played an important role in the culture of many American Indian tribes, providing both food and feathers for traditional headdresses and cloaks. Later, the Spanish conquistadors in Mexico claimed first European discovery of the wild turkey, which were domesticated and taken back to Spain around 1520. In following years, it is said – with much controversy – that the first pilgrims brought the domesticated bird with them to use as food, not knowing that turkeys already existed in large abundance in the forested lands of their new home. Whether the first pilgrims did or did not bring domesticated birds with them, it is widely known that later colonists did.

How did the turkey get its name? Turkey meat became popular when it arrived in Spain. Eventually imported to England, the American turkey was mistaken for the African guinea fowl, which was imported to Europe through the Ottoman Empire (Turkey) and came to be known as the turkey-cock or turkey-hen. Resembling the guinea fowl, the American bird was also called "turkey," and the name stuck.

In North America, overhunting and habitat destruction meant that by the early 1900s turkeys were almost nonexistent. It was estimated that by 1930 there were only about 30,000 birds in all of North America. However, through conservation efforts by state wildlife agencies and hunter conservation organizations such as the National Wild Turkey Federation (NWTF.org), turkeys have become a wonderful success story. North America now has a restored and thriving population of 7 million birds. Even Hawaii has a healthy population on its Big Island.

Biology

The North American wild turkey has five subspecies: the Eastern, Merriam's, Gould's, Rio Grande and Osceola. Another species is the colorful Ocellated turkey, which lives in the southern jungles of Mexico.

An adult male turkey is called a tom while a young male turkey is called a jake. The best way to differentiate between the two is to look at their tail feathers; the young jake's tail feathers are longer in the middle while all of the tom's feathers are even in length. Being older, a tom will also have a longer beard and spurs. The beard is a long cluster of hair-like feathers that grow from the tom's chest, and the spur is a claw used for fighting that is located on the back of each leg above the feet. Male turkeys are colorful with brown, black, white and iridescent greens. Adult females are called hens and a young hen is called a jenny. Both hens and jennys are not as colorful as their male counterparts, being mostly a drab brown color; 10-20 percent of hens can also grow beards.

Turkeys have voracious appetites, constantly feeding during active hours. Their diet includes acorns from oaks, nuts from trees like hickory, beech, pine and chestnuts, berries and a variety of seeds. Insects are a vital food source for growing young turkeys, or poults. Adults have also been observed eating small frogs, snakes and lizards.

Range & Habitat

Wild turkeys are found in all of the lower 49 states where there is open woodland habitat. Small pockets of wild turkeys are also rumored to exist in Alaska, but that's a different conversation. As turkeys are most concentrated in the eastern half of the United States, it is best to check with your state's game management agen-

Mature male turkeys, called toms, are identified by their beards and spurs.

cy if you live where turkeys are less abundant.

Open woodland habitat is best suited for the wild turkey. They also like harvested fields where they can feed on waste grain and insects, and easily watch for predators with their keen eyesight. Strutting toms are often observed by hunters in these fields, too. Overgrown forests that are not managed with prescribed burns or logging are often too thick for turkeys to feel safe.

Firearms, Archery & Equipment

Firearms

The 12-gauge shotgun is by far the most popular gun used for turkey hunting. But with better powder and ammunition on the market today, the 20 gauge can also deliver the goods to a turkey as long as you do not shoot too far – a good average for each is 40 yards maximum for a 12 gauge and 30 yards maximum for a 20 gauge – all depending on the type of ammunition and choke used. Pump shotguns are widely used, but other types such as the semiauto or double barrel will also work. Guns should be camouflaged or all black to blend in with your surroundings. If you use a traditional blued steel gun with a wood stock, make sure there are no shiny parts that can reflect sunlight and catch any unwanted attention from turkeys. If you do have any bright metal on your gun, camouflage tape will take care of that problem. A 24-inch or so barrel is a good choice as you will be maneuvering around in tight, brushy areas. Many states do not allow optical sights for turkey hunting, so an adjustable rifle-type HiViz® bead sight is a good alternative.

Ammunition

Magnum 3-inch shotshells are plenty good medicine for turkeys in both the 12 and 20 gauge. Shot sizes most used are the 4, 5 and 6, with 4 being the largest shot. Choose the shot size that works best for you and your gun and

Wild turkeys prefer open woodland habitat and can be observed in harvested fields where they feed on waste grain.

choke combination. Do you want more pellets from the 6 or more knockdown power of the 4? Both will work on a well-placed shot.

Choke

You will want a very tight shot pattern so use a specialized turkey choke at the end of your barrel, or at least a full choke. Remember, you are aiming like you would with a rifle. The target is the head and neck area of the turkey for the quickest kill and the least amount of meat damage.

Archery

The same archery gear you would use for deer is perfectly acceptable for turkey. Even though they are smaller than deer, turkeys are tough game. Hunting tactics for turkey are similar for both shotgun and archery, but the challenge in hunting with a bow is drawing back without being noticed by a turkey's keen vision.

When hunting turkeys with a bow, choose an aggressive broadhead. Many hunters like to use a mechanical broadhead instead of a fixed-

When hunting turkeys with a shotgun, aim for the head and upper neck area for a quick kill.

Male turkeys are more colorful than females, with feathers that are highlighted by brown, black, white and iridescent greens.

blade broadhead to hunt turkeys; the expanding mechanical blade offers a wider cutting diameter, which can mean the difference between dropping a bird, or losing a bird that has such a small vital area. There is a wide variety of brands and styles of broadheads available. Your best bet is to talk to a professional at an archery shop to find out which type will work best for you and your bow.

Camouflage

Unless hunting from a blind, you must be camouflaged from head to toe when turkey hunting and that includes keeping your hands and face covered, too. Pick a camo pattern that will blend in with the habitat you will be hunting and for the time of year. Greens for spring and drab colors for fall are good rules to keep in mind. If you will be hunting from a blind wear clothes that match the inside color of your blind, usually black.

Decoys

Decoys can be used in the spring when toms are in the mood to breed hens and to put eager jakes in their place. Having a hen decoy is a good start to pique a tom's interest, and having a jake decoy nearby may just get a tom to come running in. He will attempt to run off the jake decoy to claim the hen, hopefully allowing you a shot.

Calls

The four most widely used turkey calls are the box call, slate call, diaphragm call and push-style friction call. Less popular calls include the wingbone call and tube call. Each will have its own unique sound and pitch, but all are designed to achieve the same end: to attract turkeys. With a little practice, all calls can be used to produce basic hen sounds including yelps, clucks, cuts and purrs. It also doesn't hurt to be proficient with two or three styles of calls to give yourself a wider variety of sounds to work with. There are plenty of informational DVDs, CDs and In-

ternet resources available to help you become a great turkey caller.

During the spring, excited toms will often gobble at almost any sound. When in the woods, use a locator call to help you quickly figure out where the tom is, especially if you are hunting in a large area. Use a call that sounds natural to turkeys, such as a barred owl, hawk or crow call. Predator calls can work, too. If you can get the tom to gobble back it will help you save a lot of time in figuring out where to hunt.

A. The box call is operated by rubbing a paddle to the sides of a rectangular wooden box.

B. The slate call is a round, flat pot that fits in the palm of your hand, surfaced with slate, aluminum or glass. A striker is used to rub against the slate to imitate different turkey sounds.

C. The push-style friction call is the easiest call to use, perfect for beginners who can operate it by simply pushing a dowel that springs back and forth inside a box.

D. The diaphragm call is perhaps the most difficult call to use, but its hand-free operation makes it popular among more advanced turkey hunters. It is a U-shaped call that is placed between the tongue and roof of your mouth. Through the manipulation of air pressure, tongue and mouth movement, the user can produce different turkey sounds with minimal motion, lowering the chances of startling a turkey and freeing up your hands to use a shotgun or bow. Diaphragm calls are not easy to master, but will become your go-to call once you learn how to make them work for you.

Hunting

Spring is the time for breeding, and making yourself as "attractive" as possible to a male turkey is basically the game. When turkey hunting in the spring you will need to hide yourself within trees and brush. Hunt in a blind, or wear camouflage from head to toe and sit with your back against a tree or bush to conceal your outline, keeping very still. A large tree is best to

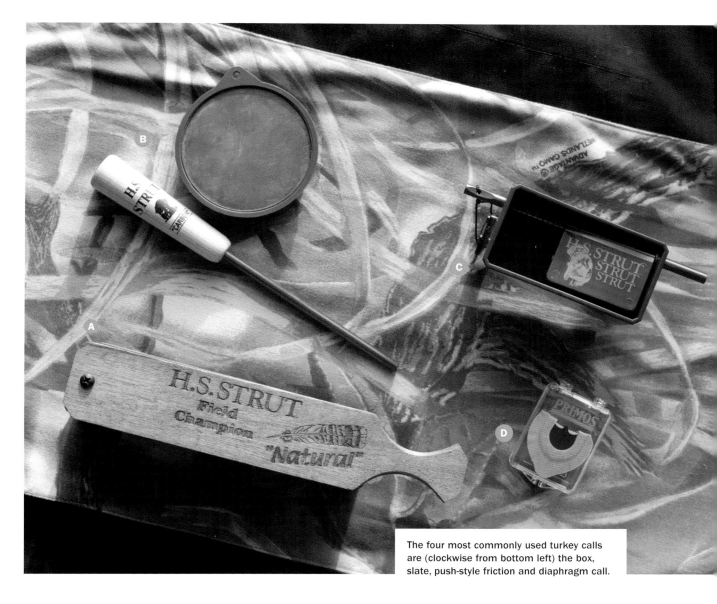

The four most commonly used turkey calls are (clockwise from bottom left) the box, slate, push-style friction and diaphragm call.

protect you from behind should another hunter mistake you for a turkey. Never wear the colors white, blue or red when turkey hunting – hunters associate these colors with a gobbler's head and can mistake you for a turkey. Try to keep the area in front of you fairly open so you will have a clear lane to shoot when a turkey is in range. Place a decoy or two within shooting range to provide the tom something to visually focus on when he approaches, about 20 to 40 yards away from you. Place the decoys too far away and he will not come within shooting range – place the decoys too closely and he or any other turkeys with him will see your movements more easily, especially if you're bow hunting.

Once you have located a tom, you will need to close the distance between you without letting him know that you are not another turkey. This is not as easy as it sounds. Turkeys have incredible hearing and eyesight, comparable to 8X

Standing Broadside

Full Strut Broadside

Full Strut Straight On

Archery Shot Placement on a Turkey

Turkeys should never be shot in the body when using a shotgun because their body feathers are too thick for pellets to effectively penetrate. Instead, aim for the head and upper neck area, which will break its neck vertebrate and quickly immobilize the bird.

When hunting turkeys with a bow, you will need to be more thoughtful on your shot placement depending on which direction the bird is facing. Turkeys are more feathers than body and their vitals are only about the size of a baseball. For a broadside shot on a standing bird, draw an imaginary horizontal line from the base of the beard, then draw another line from the thighs up. Where those two lines intersect is where you should aim. If the turkey is facing away from you, shoot for the beard line right in the middle of the back; this should break its spine and reach its vitals. If the turkey is walking toward you, shoot at the base of the beard or a little above; avoid shooting too much to the left or right of the beard to keep the breast meat intact. When and where hens are legal to shoot, imagine where her beard would be if she were a tom, and aim for the same areas.

If the tom is strutting, its feathers will puff out and stand up, making the bird look even bigger than it is. Shoot too high or too low and you will hit only feathers. Even on a strutting bird, focus on the bird's center mass by drawing a horizontal line from the beard and up from the thigh on a broadside bird. Shoot it at the base of the beard if the strutting tom is facing you. And on a classically strutting bird that is facing away from you, its tail feathers will be raised to expose its vent. Shoot straight through the vent on a strutting tom and you will reach its vitals.

binoculars. Turkeys can be exceptionally wary because of all the different predators they face in the wild. Any sound or movement that seems unnatural to them can bust your entire hunt.

Oftentimes, a tom will not be alone. He may be accompanied by other toms, jakes or hens. Other toms or jakes will mean more eyes and ears to contend with, and a hen will not like the idea of another hen (you) trying to take the tom away from her. Begin by letting out plain yelps or clucks to draw in the tom. How much you call will be up for experimentation – some toms will respond better to more calling while others like a hen that plays hard to get. If the tom is henned up, or with another hen, don't be disheartened. Try to pick a fight with the dominant hen by letting out loud, excited yelps. She will not like you competing for her tom. If you can get her to come in closer to investigate, she may bring the tom with her.

When the tom shows himself, your decoys should help seal the deal. The hen decoy will draw him in to mate and the jake decoy will draw him in to fight.

It is a good idea to hunt from a blind to conceal movement if you are a beginner or if you are a fidgety person. Blinds are also widely used by archery hunters. Even for expert hunters, drawing back a bow without being noticed by a turkey is extremely difficult. Once he is within shooting range and you are presented a clear shot, carefully draw back your bow or raise your gun without being noticed, then aim and shoot.

The fall turkey hunting season, if your state allows it, is a different hunting experience altogether and will often involve a little more chasing. Turkeys are now flocked up in groups according to sex, and in some states both toms and hens can be hunted. These flocks can be as small as a few birds, or more than a hundred. Turkeys seek to gather up during the fall for security reasons – it provides more eyes and ears on the lookout for predators.

One of the most time-honored tactics is breaking up a flock and then calling it to gather again near you. To break up a flock, sneak up close and charge into the middle of the flock with movement and noise. This will cause them to scatter in all directions. Be careful not to start your attack too soon or too far away, or the whole flock might run off together. If legal in your state, a well-trained dog can accomplish this task for you. Always remember to break up a flock with your gun safely unloaded to prevent accidents.

Once the flock has been scattered, find a good hiding spot nearby and start calling. The turkeys are now alone and frightened by what just happened. Using the assembly call, which is a yelp, start calling out to the scattered birds. They should eventually answer back and return to the area. If all goes well, the birds will return to where you are waiting for them, allowing you an opportunity to shoot.

Other tactics include watching for turkey movements and sneaking ahead to cut them off. When hunting with others, hunters can be placed in different locations to help push turkeys toward the shooter.

Field to Table

If you choose to breast out your turkey, that can be done in the field. If you choose to pluck the bird, place it in a cooler with ice until you can get it home. Place the turkey in a plastic bag to prevent it from soaking up water; moisture promotes the growth of bacteria and wet feathers can be difficult to pluck.

Cleaning: How to Breast a Turkey

Many hunters prefer to breast out turkeys because it is faster and cleaner than plucking a whole bird. We will keep the legs, too, which are also easy to remove.

STEP 1. Begin by plucking the breast feathers to expose a good area of skin. Then cut through the skin without cutting into the breast meat. Pull and peel the skin away to expose the breast underneath.

STEP 2. Carve out the breast meat by following the contours of the rib and keel bone without puncturing the body cavity.

STEP 3. With the help of your knife, peel back the skin from both legs.

STEP 4. Look for the hip joint that connects the thigh to the body. Cut off both thighs at this joint.

STEP 5. Cut off the feet and shanks at the hock joint. Rinse the breast meat and legs under cold water. Pat dry turkey pieces with paper towels before cooking or freezing.

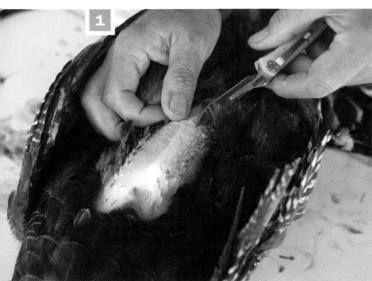

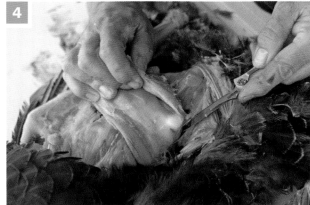

Cleaning: How to Pluck a Turkey

The steps below are for dry plucking a turkey. But if you would like to wet pluck a turkey, begin by bringing a large pot of water to a simmer. Then while holding the turkey by its feet, dunk it in the simmering water headfirst so that all of its feathers are submerged. Hold it in the water for 10 seconds and then proceed to the steps below. Make sure to begin plucking immediately after you've dunked the turkey in the hot water – wet plucking only works if the skin remains warm.

STEP 1. Begin by plucking the turkey's large wing feathers; pliers will make the job much easier. For more difficult feathers at the wing tip, snip them off with kitchen shears. Then pluck the rest of the smaller feathers on the wings.

STEP 2. Pluck the feathers on the back and sides with an upward, snapping motion of the wrist. Then pluck the breast feathers, being careful not to tear any skin. Grab only a few feathers at a time. Pluck to just above the base of the neck.

STEP 3. Pluck all of the feathers around the legs and thighs. Then pull the tail feathers straight out and clean up around the rest of the tail area.

STEP 4. Snip off the tail above the anus with kitchen shears.

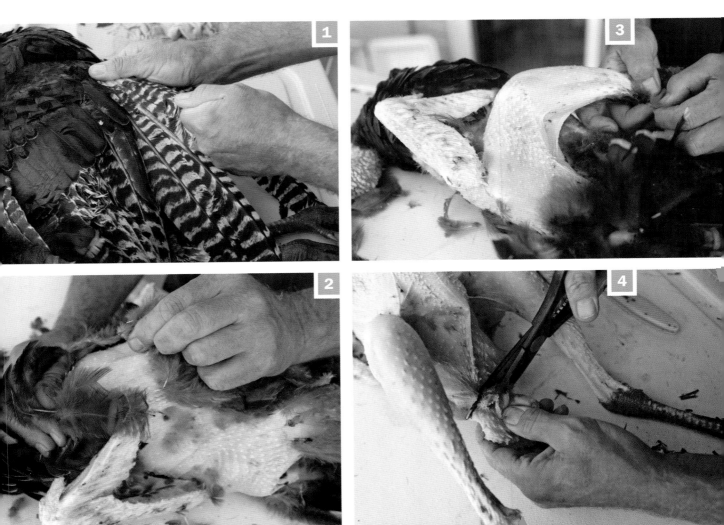

STEP 5. Cut off the head at the base of the neck.

STEP 6. Cut open the soft area below the breast to expose the innards, being careful not to puncture the intestines. Pull everything out and discard, including the crop located near the top of the breast. Gizzards and liver can be saved, if desired.

STEP 7. Cut off the feet and shanks at the hock. If there are still some small feathers left, you can singe them off with a torch (see Waterfowl chapter). Finally, rinse the bird thoroughly under cold water and pat dry with paper towels before cooking or freezing.

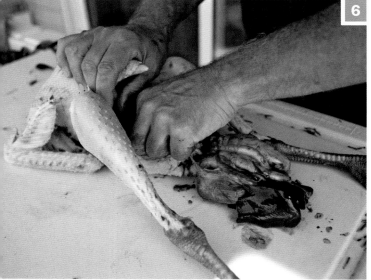

Cooking Wild Turkey

Other than outward appearance and size, wild turkeys are similar to domesticated turkeys in taste and texture. Though not as plump and tender as domestics, wild turkeys will work with most, if not all of your favorite turkey recipes for a store-bought bird. However, do adjust cooking times to compensate for their smaller size and leaner skin.

Frying Wild Turkey

To fry a whole turkey, start by rinsing it under cold water. Dab dry with paper towels, then salt the bird well inside and out. Allow it to come to room temperature; usually about an hour. Heat peanut oil to 350 degrees Fahrenheit in your fryer. Before cooking, give the turkey another good dry with paper towels and then rub it with your favorite seasonings. Carefully lower it into your fryer according to your fryer's directions for turkey, and cook for three to four minutes per pound. The breast meat should register 165 degrees on your meat thermometer when cooked. Once done, carefully remove the turkey from the oil and drain it. Tent with foil and allow the turkey to rest for 15–20 minutes before carving.

Please note that there is a give and take when

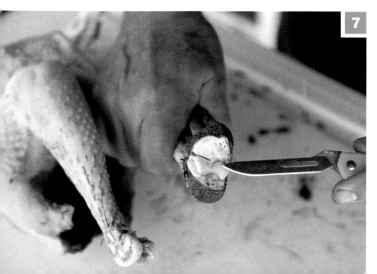

it comes to cooking a whole wild turkey. While the breast may be perfectly cooked, wild turkey legs and thighs are not as plump and tender as domestic turkeys, making them poor candidates for quick cooking methods like frying or roasting.

To make turkey fingers or nuggets, cut turkey breasts into the desired size pieces. Season the pieces with salt and your favorite spices, then dredge them in Panko breadcrumbs or your go-to fried chicken batter (see Fried Buttermilk Rabbit recipe for batter). To use Panko, lightly coat turkey pieces with flour, dip them in beaten egg and then dip into the breadcrumbs seasoned with salt and pepper. For extra-crispy Panko crusted nuggets or strips, dip the pieces in beaten egg and breadcrumbs again.

Wild turkey breasts can be roasted, grilled, fried or pan seared.

Gently press on the breadcrumbs to make sure they stick. Fry Panko or battered turkey pieces in 375-degree peanut or vegetable oil until golden brown on both sides, or about three to five minutes.

Turkey for Braising

Never throw wild turkey legs and thighs away. They are easy to remove and have plenty of meat on them. You may find that you prefer them to the breast meat. Save the legs and thighs for slow-cooking methods such as soups, stews and braises. Use the bones to make stock.

Roasting Wild Turkey

Roasting a turkey would yield similar results to a fried turkey – great breasts but rubbery legs and thighs. If you are okay with this trade-off, then roasting a whole wild turkey makes for a beautiful presentation. Due to an oven's dry heat, we highly recommend brining or injecting your wild turkey before roasting – we do this

with every domestic bird we roast for Thanksgiving and wild turkeys would greatly benefit from this as well (see brining recipe in the Waterfowl chapter). Before roasting allow the turkey to come to room temperature, and preheat the oven to 350 degrees. Meanwhile, salt the turkey inside and out, then rub softened butter and any other seasonings all over the turkey, including under the skin of the breasts. Roast an unstuffed turkey for 15 minutes per pound. If the skin starts to get too brown, tent the turkey with foil. Once done, the breast meat should be 165 degrees on your thermometer. Allow the turkey to rest for 10-15 minutes before serving.

When roasting skinless breast meat, you must be careful not to dry it out. Without the protection of skin there is nothing to keep the breast moist. Wrap the breasts in bacon and bake at 375 degrees for 30 minutes to counteract this lack of fat. Or you can brine it, or try our turkey in parchment paper recipe, and its ingredients can be substituted with anything you like.

Turkey Legs Noodle Soup with Fennel

Servings: 4-6
Prep Time: 10 mins
Cook Time: 1 hr & 45 mins

2 wild turkey legs and thighs

7 cups of water

2 carrots, peeled and diced

2 celery stalks, diced

¼ of a medium onion, diced

1 teaspoon of kosher salt, or to taste

¼ teaspoon of white pepper

½ teaspoon of coriander

¼ teaspoon of Hungarian paprika

1 generous pinch of dried thyme

2 teaspoons of fresh parsley, chopped

2 cups of egg noodles, uncooked

3 to 5 fronds of fennel

1. Place turkey legs and thighs in a large pot with seven cups of water. Bring to a boil then simmer for 30 minutes, covered. Take out the legs and thighs and shred the meat with forks, reserving the bones. Set the meat aside and return the bones to the broth and simmer for an additional 45 minutes, covered.

2. Remove the bones and discard. Add chopped carrots, onion, celery and shredded turkey meat into the broth, followed by white pepper, coriander, salt, paprika, parsley and a pinch of thyme. Simmer for 10 minutes.

3. Then increase the heat and add egg noodles. Cook until tender, following the package directions and stirring occasionally. During the last five minutes of cooking add the fennel fronds and simmer. Then remove and discard the fronds. Make sure the vegetables are tender. Adjust the seasonings then serve soup with crusty bread or crackers.

Save wild turkey legs
for soups, stews and braises.

Turkey in Parchment
with Cherry Tomatoes and Tarragon

1. Preheat the oven to 400 degrees. Sprinkle salt and pepper all over the turkey breasts and allow them to come to room temperature. In a bowl combine olive oil, the minced garlic and shallot, tarragon, sugar snap peas, tomatoes and a generous pinch of salt and pepper.

2. Cut two pieces of parchment paper 12 inches by 16 inches. Place half of the tomato and pea mixture in the middle of one piece of parchment and then lay one turkey breast on top. Sprinkle half of the parsley and one tablespoon of butter on top of the turkey. Splash in some wine then meet the two short ends together and fold over 1 inch. Fold over a couple more times then crimp up the sides to make half-moon packets. Repeat with the other turkey breast.

3. Bake in the oven for 30 minutes, or until the breasts are cooked through. Allow guests to open up their own packets and slide contents onto their plates, then discard parchment. Serve with rice. If you want to make a pan sauce, melt two tablespoons of butter and sauté one minced shallot and one minced clove of garlic. Deglaze the pan with a splash of white wine, then pour in the juice from the turkey packets. Bring to a boil and allow it to reduce to the desired thickness.

Servings: 2
Prep Time: 45 mins
Cook Time: 40 mins

2 skinless and boneless
  wild turkey breasts

kosher salt and pepper, to taste

6 ounces of sugar snap peas

1 cup of cherry tomatoes, halved

2 tablespoons of olive oil

2 leaves of fresh or dried tarragon,
  chopped

3 cloves of garlic, minced

2 large shallots, thinly sliced

white wine

2 tablespoons of butter

1 tablespoon of fresh parsley,
  chopped

Special equipment: parchment paper

Turkey breast baked in a parchment paper packet with cherry tomatoes, sugar snap peas, fresh herbs and a splash of wine.

Bobwhite quail are the most widely hunted quail species in the United States.

CHAPTER 6

QUAIL

There are six species of quail in North America including the California quail, mountain quail, scaled quail, Gambel's quail, Montezuma quail and the most common species of all, the northern bobwhite quail. A fine and delicate white meat, quail are one of the most tasty and tender game birds around, and quite difficult to shoot at that. The earliest record of white man eating bobwhites occurred in 1557 when Spanish explorer and conquistador Hernando de Soto's expedition received a gift of turkeys and partridges (most likely bobwhite quail) at an American Indian village located in present-day Georgia.

Biology

Though small, quail are supremely handsome birds. The males of the mountain, California and Gambel's quail have a mostly bluish-gray breast and back feathers with brown, white, and black scaled belly feathers. A striking face that is mostly black outlined with a white stripe, Gambel's and California males have a brown cap on top of their heads. Males of all three species have tufts of feathers rising from their crowns and Mountain quail's are slightly forked.

The scaled quail looks just like its name implies, a fully scaled appearance of brown, black and white feathers, with a light brown head. The Montezuma quail is fully scaled as well, but with a striking, patterned head of black, light brown and off-white. The females of each species look similar to their male counterparts though not as flashy or distinct.

Each species lays clutches of nine to 15 eggs in the spring. Under good conditions, a pair may have two to three clutches per year. The chicks grow quickly and will leave the nest after a few hours. They attempt their first flight around 10 days after hatching.

Quail tend to live with a multitude of other quail, sometimes numbering 15-80 birds or more. During mating season these coveys will break apart as birds pair up. After the eggs have hatched coveys tend to reform and sometimes birds will raise their young communally. A wild quail rarely lives beyond 1½ years, but in captivity they have lived more than 5 years.

Quails are heavily preyed upon by coyotes, snakes, foxes, cats, hawks, owls and bobcats, among others. But like many other wild animals today, habitat loss is their biggest threat.

Range & Habitat

California quail are found throughout California, north into British Columbia and eastward to Nevada and parts of Idaho. Mountain quail range from southern California north to the Oregon and Washington border, living at higher elevations within that range; there are small enclaves of mountain quail in western Nevada as well.

Gambel's quail are found mostly in the Southwest and are most abundant in Arizona. They also call some deserts of southern California, New Mexico and a few small areas of southern Utah and Nevada home.

Montezuma quail only inhabit West Texas and a small section along the borders of southern Arizona and New Mexico. More abundant in that area is the scaled quail, which inhabits the western half of Texas, southwest Colorado, New Mexico and southeast Arizona.

The northern bobwhite quail covers roughly half of the United States. Its range spans from eastern Colorado and New Mexico to the Atlantic Ocean, and from Florida north to Michigan.

All species of quail, except one, prefer fairly open landscapes. In semi-arid western areas the California, Gambel's, Montezuma and scaled quail like sagebrush and chaparral areas. Bobwhites like a grassland-forb-shrub habitat, where half of the land is exposed and the rest is composed of woody and herbaceous vegetation. Only the mountain quail prefers the dense, shrubby brush habitat found in the coniferous forests of the major mountain ranges of the West. Mountain quail tend to migrate up and down the mountains as the seasons change.

Firearms & Ammunition

As with all upland hunting, the shotgun is the tool of choice to hunt quail, with everything from a 12 gauge to a .410 being used. In fact, smaller gauges such as the 20 and 28 are suitable because they are lightweight and easier to carry during long hikes over difficult terrain. The .410 bore is best reserved as a gun for an advanced shooter; it is the smallest round and therefore has the least amount of shot inside it. Still, the 12 gauge remains the most popular size and can throw the most shot downrange. However, it is also heavier and may not always be the best for what tends to be fast-action shooting.

All shotgun actions are used for quail hunting. The pump shotgun is known for its versatility, the semiauto shotgun is popular for its quickness on follow-up shots and the double-barrel shotgun, both the over/under and the side-by-side, will always be a traditional mainstay. Although the single shot is rarely used, it is a good choice for beginners because it forces them to learn how to aim well and

The over/under is a classic gun for quail hunting.

take advantage of that one shot. It is also a lighter gun to carry. Whichever gauge you choose, aim for a lightweight model as it will make your day more enjoyable in the field.

A 2¾-inch shotshell is the best choice. Additionally, shot size 7½ or 8 is best. Some hunters will also use number 9 shot, but a marginally hit bird will most likely escape. Quail are good runners and can be difficult to find once they hit the ground on the run and hide in surrounding cover. The use of a good retrieving dog is a huge help for these types of situations.

Hunting

Similar to pheasant hunting, quail hunting will take some time to learn and master. As with any type of hunting, it is always better to find an experienced friend or mentor who can show you what to look for in the field. Join an orga-

nization such as Quail Forever (quailforever.org) by looking for a local chapter in your area. Not only will these folks have seasoned hunters in their ranks, they also do fantastic conservation work to benefit quail.

Before You Hunt

As we hinted at previously, quail hunting involves a lot of walking. Make sure you wear a pair of comfortable, broken-in boots, because a blister will definitely cut your day afield short. You should also wear blaze orange when hunting, which many states require. Even if your state doesn't, we highly recommend wearing it anyway for safety's sake in the fast action of a quail hunt — a blaze orange hat and vest will do. Lastly, a good pair of brush pants or chaps will be appreciated at the end of the day. They will save your pants and legs from thick and thorny brush.

Don't forget to keep yourself and your dog hydrated while hunting. *Photo credit: NEBRASKAland Magazine*

Also be sure to bring plenty of water and snacks for both you and your dog whether your hunt is during hot or cold weather. For additional advice on equipment see information for pheasant hunting in Chapter 8.

Oftentimes, being a successful quail hunter means putting in the research time before the actual hunt. Before you head out to the field, find out what kind of quail are in your area and read up on the type of habitat they prefer. Read the information that's available on your state's game department website and hunting brochures, and don't be afraid to give them a call to learn about quail populations in the area you plan to hunt. You may be surprised by how much information they can give you to help you get started.

Chasing Birds

Once you have arrived at your chosen location, try to walk with your face into the wind. If you're hunting with a dog this will allow it to catch the scent of birds and then to track and locate them. If possible, look for quail tracks and listen for their distinctive call. Each species of quail has a different call — a quick visit to the Internet will bring up many sound samples to listen to. Try to stay quiet when hunting quail, as a lot of noise will alert them to your presence and cause them to cease their activity.

Calling quail is a lot of fun and can be done with man-made instruments. If you know there are quail around, enter the area quietly and wait patiently for several minutes. Once you feel like your presence has been forgotten, you can begin to call. The calls will reassure quail in the area that all is

When chasing quail, watch the terrain. When quail are cornered or faced with a drop-off where they are uncomfortable to run, they may be forced to flush.

well, encouraging them to resume their activity and calling, which might help you locate them in the field.

Once you locate a covey, they will usually do one of two things. The first is that they will run away from you. Quail are very fast runners that would rather run than fly. If that happens, pick up your stride to keep up with them. Watch the terrain and you may be able to get them cornered in a ravine or a drop-off where they feel uncomfortable and can't run, forcing them to flush. They will suddenly explode in flight with several birds taking off in different directions at once. Even for the seasoned hunter this can be a heart-stopping surprise. It's vital to keep your cool and stay focused. Pick one bird, focus on it and shoot.

The second possibility is that you will approach some brush that you have seen or heard birds enter. They tend to hold extremely tight at times like this. Be patient and the birds may get nervous enough to flush right from your feet.

Hunting with Dogs

Good upland hunting dogs can help hunters locate, flush and or retrieve birds, depending on the breed. Hunters might use a single dog or a couple to work together, such as a pointer and a retriever. There are many, many excellent gun dog breeds such as the Brittany, other span-

German shorthaired pointers, like Remington, are excellent upland bird dogs.

iels, English pointer, English setter, golden retriever, Labrador retriever, German shorthaired pointer, Vizsla and more. If you're looking for a new hunting partner do some research and visit a kennel that specializes in training and breeding hunting dogs. They can help you pick a suitable breed based on your needs, and teach you how to work with your dog at home and in the field.

Field to Table

Once you get birds on the ground, cool them down as soon as possible. Depending on where you hunt, high temperatures can promote spoilage. At the earliest chance, clean the birds. Quail should not be breasted out. Being so small they are best cooked and eaten whole.

Cleaning

Quail can be dry plucked or wet plucked. Dry plucking takes much more time and leaves behind thin, wispy feathers that can take even more time to remove. Quail skin is really thin so dry plucking can cause tearing, but if done correctly the end result will look clean. Wet plucking is much faster and is a great method to avoid tears. However, you risk the chance of slightly cooking the skin if the water is too hot or if you leave the bird in for too long.

Dry Plucking

STEP 1. Begin by plucking the wing feathers, pulling out only a couple at a time.

STEP 2. Pluck the body feathers. Again, only pluck a couple feathers at a time because quail skin tears so easily. It helps to use your thumb to anchor down the skin to keep it from tearing.

Quail are difficult to dry pluck without tearing any skin.

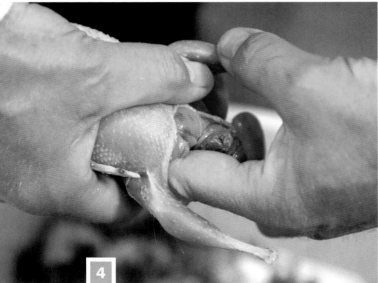

STEP 3. Use kitchen shears to snip off the head and feet.

STEP 4. To gut, snip off the tail. Using one or two fingers, reach into the body cavity and pull out the organs and intestines. Finally, clean and rinse out the body. Dab dry with paper towels before freezing.

Wet Plucking

STEP 1. Heat enough water in a pot to immerse an entire bird, until it's scalding and steamy, but not boiling. Holding a bird by its feet, fully dunk the quail into the hot water and hold it there for five seconds. Raise it out of the water and allow most of the water to drain off. Do this twice more so that the bird has been dunked for a total of 15 seconds.

STEP 2. Pluck the bird while it's still warm. Only work on one bird at a time because this method only works while the feathers and skin remain warm.

STEP 3. Use kitchen shears to snip off the head, feet and tail. Then gut as described in the previous section.

Cooking Quail

Quail are like small chickens, composed of delicate white meat and thin, flavorful skin. They take to marinades very well and are easy to cook, especially over an open fire. Two to three quails will do per person, depending on their size. A mild-tasting meat, quails are easy to eat, especially to those new to wild game. Keep in mind that quail are not exactly a good first date meal. They must be devoured with bare, willing hands.

Roasting Quail

Roasting quail takes little time in a very hot oven. Simply rub oil or butter over the birds, then salt and pepper, and roast in the broiler on high for 10–15 minutes; five minutes with breast down, two to three minutes with the breast up, and one minute on each side. From start to finish, 10 minutes will give you succulent, slightly pink meat, while 15 minutes will bring the meat to well done. Get creative by using different rubs, spices and marinades to season your quails.

Grilling Quail

The way we grill quail is very similar to the way we roast it, except the process is reversed; the heat on a broiler comes from above while the heat in a grill is below. Season, marinate or brine quails as desired, then grill for 10–15 minutes; five minutes on the back, two to three minutes on the breast and one minute on each wing. Or, you can flatten the quails and cook them for five minutes on the bone side and two or three minutes on the skin side. This sequence will give you slightly pink meat.

Vietnamese-Style Roasted Quail

Servings: 2
Prep Time: 2 hrs & 10 mins
Cooking Time: about 10 mins

4 whole quails

2 tablespoons of soy sauce

2 tablespoons of Ponzu sauce

4 teaspoons of sugar

1 teaspoon of five-spice powder

1 teaspoon of freshly grated ginger

3 tablespoons of Shaoxing rice cooking wine (or dry sherry)

1 green onion, white and light green parts chopped

kosher salt, to taste

1 tablespoon of cooking oil

Dipping Sauce

1 tablespoon of lemon juice

½ teaspoon of salt

1 teaspoon of cracked black pepper

1. In a small bowl combine the soy sauce, Ponzu, sugar, five-spice, ginger, rice wine and green onion. Rinse quails under cold water and pat dry with paper towels, then rub generously with salt inside and out. Pour soy sauce mixture into a resealable zip-lock bag and add quails. Rub to distribute marinade and refrigerate for two hours.

2. Turn broiler on to high. Oil the grates on a rack in a roast pan and place it in the oven to heat up. Once the oven and pan are heated, remove the quails from the marinade and paint with olive oil or butter, then roast for five minutes breast down. Flip the quails breast up and roast for another two to three minutes, or until their skin turns golden. Finally, turn them over on their wings and roast for one minute on each side. Combine dipping sauce ingredients and serve on the side. This recipe is also perfect for grilling and frying.

Spiced quail served Vietnamese-style with a lemon, pepper and salt dipping sauce.

Grilled Quail Over Greek Salad

1. Rinse quails with cold water. Using kitchen shears, cut down the spine of each quail, then flatten them by gently cracking the wishbone. Pat the birds dry with paper towels, then generously salt both sides. Whisk together marinade ingredients and pour in a zip-lock bag along with quails. Marinate for at least two hours and up to four hours in the refrigerator.

2. Prepare the grill and cook the quails bone side down for five minutes, then two or three minutes on the skin side, or until golden and cooked through.

3. Serve with your favorite Greek salad recipe.

Servings: 2
Prep Time: 2-4 hrs
Cooking Time: 10-15 mins

4 whole quails

kosher salt

Marinade
¼ cup of olive oil

juice from 2 lemons

4 cloves of garlic, minced

1 tablespoon of flat leaf parsley, chopped

1½ teaspoons each of freshly chopped oregano, rosemary, thyme, basil and mint

2 generous pinches of salt

Grilled quail
marinated in lemon and fresh herbs served over Greek salad.

A mourning dove loafing on a tree limb during midday.

CHAPTER 7

DOVE

More ammunition is probably used during dove season than any other hunting season of the year. A small, fast bird that can travel up to 55 mph, doves can spin, dip and dive in the air, and just far enough out of range that they can leave many a veteran hunter scratching their head.

Opening day of dove season begins in late summer and is a great opportunity for hunters to sharpen their wing-shooting skills. It is also a social event in many regions to herald in the new hunting season, enjoyed every year as a tradition by family and friends. Doves are also a great way to introduce kids to the sport of hunting. A rich, dark meat, doves provide a unique and tasty table fare.

Biology

It is estimated that approximately 450 million doves live in North America. Prolific breeders, doves will sometimes nest upward of six times per year and are found throughout the continent, assuring plenty of dove hunting opportunities for sportsmen. Though there are more subspecies in the dove family, we will look at the three most common in North America: the Mourning Dove, White-winged Dove and the invasive Eurasian Collared Dove.

Mourning Doves are identified by a delicate brown to buffy-tan color with black spots on the wings and black-bordered white tips on long, pointed tail feathers. Their coloration matches

their open-country surroundings. Most people recognize Mourning Doves by their mournful, soft, drawn-out calls.

The Eurasian Collared Dove announces its presence with a three-part coo. It is larger than the Mourning Dove and is colored with chalky light brown to gray-buff feathers, broad white patches on the tail and dark wingtips. Eurasians are marked by a narrow black crescent around the nape of the neck. First introduced to the Caribbean Islands in the 1970s, the Eurasian Collared Dove has since migrated to Florida and now throughout most of the United States. Like so many invasive species its population has exploded, and in some areas they can be hunted

TOP: Mourning doves are buffy-tan colored with long, pointed tail feathers. BOTTOM: The 12-gauge shotgun is the most widely used firearm to hunt doves.

year-round with no bag limit.

The White-winged Dove is found in the southern United States. It is also slightly larger than the Mourning Dove, with a similar brown to buffy-tan coloration. It is identified by a square tail, long, thin bill, a dark line on the cheek and a white stripe at the edge of folded wings.

Doves are seed and grain eaters, which explains why they concentrate in rural farm areas. Grass seeds and cultivated grains such as barley, rye, millet, milo and oats are some of their favorites. Doves also prefer wild sunflower seeds and have been observed eating insects. While cleaning one particular dove we found so much corn spilling out of its crop and gizzard that it was a wonder it could still fly!

Range & Habitat

Doves can be found from Central America to Canada and have even been spotted in Alaska. They prefer warm weather, and when temperatures drop doves will head south for better climates. They are abundant in agricultural regions where food, water and habitat are plentiful.

Doves prefer open areas such as grasslands and cultivated fields. Their population has increased with the cutting of woodland areas, which has opened up more of their desired habitat. They are commonly seen perched on power lines and fences during the daytime after spending the morning eating and collecting gravel. Like many birds, doves must collect gravel in order to grind up and digest food in their gizzard. They are also very common in cities and towns where they can find everything they need.

Firearms & Ammunition

Give doves a moderate wind and they can pull off acrobatic moves that leave many shooters with a pile of spent shells and nothing to show for their efforts. There's around 45 million doves (only 10 percent of the entire population) taken each year, so multiply the number of rounds it takes you to down a limit of doves, and it's easy to imagine the staggering amount of ammunition that is sold for dove hunting alone.

The 12-gauge shotgun is the most widely used firearm to hunt doves. Its larger shells hold a greater amount of shot that increases your odds of a hit. Still, smaller gauges can be ideal too, as they allow the hunter a lighter, quicker mounting process when the birds come flying by. The 20 gauge's recoil is lighter than the 12, which is a good thing considering the amount of shooting you may be doing when hunting doves. The 28 gauge also gains its popularity by allowing shooters the ability to quickly point and acquire fast-moving targets. In able hands, the .410 bore is a light gun that can also be effective. Depend-

ing on where you hunt and whom you are hunting with, carrying a lighter shotgun may make your hunt a little more enjoyable.

Pumps, double barrels and even single shots are brought out to shoot doves. But, we think the best action is the semiauto shotgun, which allows for fast follow-ups with a second or third shot.

Close-range, fast-action shooting happens a lot when dove hunting so the choke on your shotgun should have a wide pattern, such as the improved cylinder. It does not take a lot of shot to down a dove, so the more open pattern you use, the better your chances of hitting them. Many hunters even use a skeet pattern.

Shot sizes 7½ and 8 are by far the most popular for dove hunting. These smaller shot sizes are ideal because they allow for a dense shot pattern, giving you approximately 350 (7½) to 410 (8) pellets in a 1-ounce load of shot in your shell. Larger shot is unnecessary because the dove is a small bird and not particularly tough. Use 2¾-inch shells for the least amount of recoil with plenty of killing power.

Hunting

For dove hunting, as with most wild game, it pays to do some preseason scouting. Doves will almost always use the same flyways as they go from their morning roost to feeding areas, then to water and back to roost in the evening. If it's been a dry year find yourself a good watering hole, as it will become a magnet to these birds. In wet years it may be more desirable to look for active feeding areas to set up near. Keep a good pair of binoculars in your vehicle so you can look from afar to follow dove travel routes across fields. Doves are most active in the mornings before 9 a.m. and in the late afternoon and evenings after 3 p.m. They will usually rest and loaf around or stay perched during the midday hours. Water is vitally important to doves, but if you can't get to the watering holes look for areas where they feed and roost.

Gary Bottger (center) and Rick Wheatley, wearing camouflage and drab colors, wait for doves by a watering hole.

Gary Bottger and his German shorthaired pointer, Hope, hunt for doves in northeast Nebraska.

In agricultural areas, don't be afraid to knock on doors and ask permission to hunt. Once given permission, always remember to pick up after yourself and others, and never, ever shoot toward buildings or livestock. Though these rules may seem like common sense, they are two of the most common issues with landowners, and can understandably prompt them to close their land to dove hunters. Be responsible and remember to thank the landowner for the opportunity to hunt. You just might receive another invite for next year.

Once you have found your location to hunt, wear some camouflage and set up in a place that will break up your outline. Even drab-colored clothes such as olives and browns will help you blend in with your surroundings. A small folding chair is nice, as dove hunting is usually a wait-

ing game. Birds may come in singles, pairs or large flocks. When a flock comes to you, do not be fooled into thinking that you can just shoot into the whole flock and drop multiple birds – this does not work. Focus on a single bird with each shot for the best chance at bringing anything home. We recommend practicing at a trap or skeet range prior to going out dove hunting. If you can afford to, it may be beneficial to get professional shooting instruction.

Most of the time you will be hunting over grass fields or uncut fields of grain. A dog is a wonderful help to retrieve downed doves. Even in short grass it can be extremely frustrating to find downed birds as they blend in with the ground so well. If you are without a dog, shoot one bird at a time and mark where it fell. Retrieve the bird immediately, never taking your eyes off that spot as you walk toward it. Once you've found your dove, return back to your spot and continue to hunt.

Dove decoys can also offer some advantage, and they're usually more effective for solo hunters or small groups, when hunter numbers are not available to provide enough field coverage. Decoys can help to lure in doves from all over the field within shooting range.

Field to Table

Dove meat is dark, sweet and rich. For such small birds they pack a big flavor and are a treat for late summer and early fall meals. Many hunters simply breast out their doves, but we recommend plucking them. They are very easy to pluck. You will be surprised by how much more satisfying it is to eat a whole dove than just the breasts.

Before we start talking about cooking, taking good care of doves in the field is just as important. Doves are small and light, making them easy to carry in your hunting vest. Get them cleaned as soon as possible and keep them relatively cool until you do. Do not let them get wet, and do not leave them in a warm vehicle or forgotten in your hunting vest.

Cleaning: How to Pluck a Dove

STEP 1. To dry pluck doves begin with plucking the wings. Pull the longer flight feathers straight out, while the smaller feathers at the top edge of the wing should be plucked in the opposite direction.

STEP 2. Pluck the feathers from the dove's breast with an upward motion. Pluck partially up the neck, but stop where you plan to cut the head off.

STEP 3. Pluck all the feathers from the back and around the thighs. Pull the tail feathers straight out.

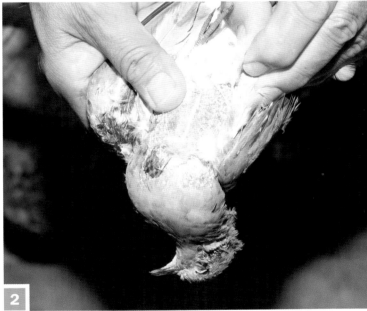

STEP 4. Snip off the feet and legs at the joint below the thighs with kitchen shears.

STEP 5. Cut off the head below the crop (you may feel seeds and grain inside) and above the breast.

STEP 6. Cut off the tail. This will allow you to pull out the dove's organs.

STEP 7. Stick one finger in the body cavity. Move your finger around to loosen the innards from the inside walls, then pull everything out and discard. Run cold water through the body cavity and rinse the dove thoroughly. Dry the dove with paper towels before freezing or cooking.

Cleaning: How to Breast a Dove

If you're in a hurry or need to clean your doves out in the field, breasting is the way to go. Begin by plucking the feathers from the breast. Then feel for the point where the breast and keel bone ends and push your thumb underneath, breaking through the skin so that your thumb is now inside the body cavity and underneath the sternum. Anchor your index finger at the top of the breast and then peel the whole breast upwards and away from the dove's back. Twist to detach the wings and the head so that you're just left with the breast (with the bone still intact). Rinse with cold water to help remove any blood or organs. Cook the breasts whole, or cut them from the breastbone to make dove poppers.

Cooking Dove

Doves are best cooked fast and hot, such as grilling, roasting, pan searing or deep-frying. They require no special treatment, but should not be overcooked. You want them to be slightly pink in the middle, which will keep them juicy and flavorful. Season doves with whatever spices you like and remember to always season well with salt before cooking.

Dove breasts can be cut away from the bone to make dove poppers.

How to Grill Doves

To grill whole doves, rub olive oil all over them and season. Stuff the cavity with fresh herbs and or lemon slices, then grill them breast up for five minutes over clean, hot grates with the lid closed. Paint bacon fat or butter over the breasts, then turn them so they are breast down and cook for two minutes, or until breasts are golden brown. Next turn the doves on their sides to get some color on the wings, one or two minutes each side. Allow them to rest for five minutes tented in foil before serving.

To grill breasted doves, marinate and season the breasts as desired. Grill for two minutes on each side. You can grill them with the bone or without the bone.

How to Fry Doves

The best way to fry whole doves is to flatten them first, to allow for more even cooking. Do this by cutting along their backs with kitchen shears. With the open cavity facing you, gently bend the sternum toward you until you feel a soft crack, which will break the wishbone and flatten the bird. Dredge flattened doves in your favorite fried chicken batter and seasonings. Heat oil to 375 degrees Fahrenheit and deep-fry doves in batches for three to four minutes, or until crispy and golden.

How to Roast Doves

We also like to roast doves under the broiler, which is an easy substitution for grilling. Season and oil doves the same way you would for grilling. Place them on a roasting pan breast down (away from the heat source) and broil on low for five minutes. Then turn them over, breast up (facing the heat source) and brush some bacon fat or butter on the breasts. Turn the broiler up to high and cook for two minutes, or until they are golden brown. Turn the doves on their sides and cook for another minute on each side to give the wings some color. If you flatten the doves, you can skip turning them on their sides.

Brown Sugar Glazed Dove Poppers

Servings: 3-4 appetizers
Prep Time: 1 hr

10 doves, breasted

1 package of bacon

2 jalapenos

2 ounces of cream cheese

Marinade

2 tablespoons of olive oil

1 tablespoon of red wine vinegar

1 clove of garlic, minced

½ teaspoon of rosemary, chopped

1 pinch of freshly ground
   black pepper

1 generous pinch of kosher salt

Brown Sugar Glaze

3 tablespoons of packed brown sugar

½ teaspoon of ground nutmeg

½ teaspoon of ground cinnamon

1½ teaspoons of water

1. Remove the breast halves from the breastbone with a small, sharp knife. Then gently flatten the breasts with a mallet between two sheets of plastic wrap. Whisk together marinade ingredients in a medium bowl. Add the dove breasts then cover the bowl and refrigerate it for at least 30 minutes.

2. Prepare the grill to medium heat. Cut the jalapenos in half lengthwise and remove the core and seeds. Then cut the jalapeno halves into matchsticks. Next, take the breasts out of the marinade and place a jalapeno stick and a little bit of cream cheese in the center of each breast. Roll everything up with slices of bacon (cut into thirds or fourths) and secure with toothpicks.

3. Grill the dove poppers until the bacon is cooked on all sides. Mix the brown sugar glaze ingredients and brush it on the poppers toward the end of grilling.

Sweet & salty
dove breasts with jalapeno and cream cheese rolled in bacon.

Fried Whole Doves
with Sweet and Sour Sauce

1. Cut through the back of the doves with kitchen shears. With the inside cavity facing you, bend the dove to flatten it – you will hear a crack. Sprinkle salt all over the doves, then leave them on the counter for 30 minutes, covered.

2. In a shallow bowl mix the flour, season salt, paprika, black pepper, thyme and cayenne pepper. Add one tablespoon of milk to the batter. Mix with a fork to form lumps.

3. Heat vegetable oil to 375 degrees. While the oil is heating up combine sweet and sour sauce ingredients in a small saucepan. Bring to a boil, then lower heat to a simmer. Whisk continuously until mixture thickens and becomes translucent in five to 10 minutes.

4. Pour one cup of milk in a shallow dish. Run the doves through the milk to wet, then dredge them in the batter mixture. Deep-fry the doves for three to four minutes or until golden brown; do not overcrowd. Drain the fried doves on paper towels.

Servings: 2
Prep Time: 30 mins
Cooking Time: 5 mins

4 whole doves

kosher salt, to taste

1 cup of milk

vegetable oil for frying

Batter
1 cup of all-purpose flour

1½ teaspoons of season salt

¼ teaspoon of Hungarian paprika (or regular)

¼ teaspoon of ground black pepper

¼ teaspoon of dried thyme

¼ teaspoon of cayenne pepper

1 tablespoon of milk

Sweet and Sour Sauce
6 tablespoons of white sugar

6 teaspoons of white vinegar

1/3 cup of water

2 tablespoons of soy sauce

1½ teaspoons of ketchup

1 tablespoon of corn starch

1 teaspoon of freshly ground ginger

1 teaspoon of Sambal Oelek Fresh Chili Paste, or to taste

Fried whole doves served with sweet and sour sauce is an Asian and Southern fusion.

Unlike brown-colored females, male ring-necked pheasants are characterized by colorful plumage with a red face and long tails.

CHAPTER 8

PHEASANT

Ring-necked pheasants come from Asia, most notably China. In 1881 the United States Consul General to China, Owen Nickerson Denny, shipped 60 birds to Washington state for release in the Columbia River area. Although unclear, it is assumed that this first transplant was unsuccessful, but in 1882 and 1884 more birds were introduced into the Willamette Valley area of Oregon where the Dennys had a homestead. This transplant was wildly successful. So successful in fact, that in 1892 Oregon held its first hunting season for pheasants where 50,000 birds were taken. It did not take long for those birds to spread into Washington, and by this point other states had seen the adaptability of pheasants and the great sport that they offered, spurring the release of ring-necked pheasants in approximately 40 other states. In 1943 South Dakota named the pheasant its state bird.

Since then, pheasant hunting in the United States has become a favorite outdoor tradition. Talk to many older hunters and they'll fondly tell stories of traveling from farm to farm, hunting pheasants with family before lunch on Thanksgiving or Christmas day. Walk into many small-town Midwest taverns and you'll find neon Budweiser signs outlining the shapes of running roosters. If you're going to take up hunting, you should pheasant hunt at least once in your lifetime. The excitement of following behind eager, hard-working dogs, the heart-stopping moment when a rooster flushes in front of you, and the hurrah in dropping your first bird from the sky is an experience that will never be forgotten.

Biology

Starting at the head, the male ring-neck's feathers are an iridescent blue-green with a crisp white "ring" around the base of its neck. A dramatic red wattle adorns his face, which surrounds the eyes. The body is a shimmering gold-brown-bronze combination with a splashes of a lighter blue-gray and purples in the wings and rump area. From this rump area, the tail feathers turn from a rust color into a pointed fan of brown and black bars, around 20 or more inches long. A beautiful bird indeed, it is impossible to accurately describe all the different patterns and colors that exist on one male ring-necked pheasant.

Rio, a pointing Labrador retriever, brings a prized rooster back to the hunter.

The female is a more subdued dark and light brown, with a black and white mottled pattern that helps her stay hidden in the covers where she tends to her eggs and chicks. The overall length of a rooster can be as much as 35 inches, its tail making up half that length, but a hen tends to be smaller.

Range & Habitat

In North America pheasants range where farmland is abundant, specifically farmland with plenty of edge cover for nesting. These birds are found from the Pacific Northwest in states such as Washington and Oregon to the central valley of California. Skip the Rocky Mountains and look to the grasslands of Idaho, Montana, Wyoming, Colorado and all of the Great Plains states up into the plains of Canada, then follow the farmlands of the upper Midwest into several of the New England states. If you don't live in or near the pheasant's range, look into "put-and-take" pheasant clubs, which are widespread across the United States. They usually offer longer seasons than public-land regulations allow.

Pheasants are creatures of the open plains and farmland. They usually live out their entire lives within a home range of one square mile, preferring nesting cover, brood habitat, winter cover and food all in close proximity. Some preferred food sources include corn, milo, barley, oats, wheat, sunflower and insects. In addition to blocks of grassland, prime pheasant habitat may include some wetlands and wooded areas. Shelterbelts, overgrown fence lines, windbreaks and abandoned farmsteads are also useful to pheasants.

The availability of nesting cover is the single most important factor in determining whether a population will increase or decrease. Ideal nesting cover should be composed of a mixture of both cool and warm season grasses, provide proper concealment from predators, protection from weather and remain relatively free from human disturbance. Some of the best nesting cover can also double as brood habitat.

According to Pheasants Forever, roadsides can also provide important grassland habitat, contributing up to five acres of potential nesting cover along each mile of rural Midwest roads. In some areas, 40 percent of pheasants in the fall population are produced around roadsides – something to think about while you're driving by roadsides that are mowed or burned too often.

Hunting

While we can provide you with tips and hints on how to hunt pheasants, nothing beats first-hand instruction from a friend or experienced hunter who can show you the more intricate points of pheasant hunting, especially when hunting behind dogs. A good place to start is to join your local Pheasants Forever chapter (pheasantsforever.org), where you will meet like-minded people who are passionate about pheasant hunting as well as conserving the land for the benefit of these birds.

Firearms

The most popular shotgun for pheasant hunting is the 12 gauge, with the 20 gauge gaining more popularity in recent years. Anything smaller and you have a higher chance of wounding or crippling a bird rather than killing it. Any action will work depending on your personal preference, but the over/under is one of the most popular among dedicated pheasant hunters because it allows the option of two different choke sizes when chasing this speedy bird. But in pure numbers alone, the pump action still holds supreme, while the semiauto is quickly growing in popularity, able to handle the furious action that can happen in the field. The semiauto's operation also reduces some of the felt recoil.

Shot sizes 5 or 6 will do just fine. These are the traditional shot sizes and they work as well as they ever have with today's upgrades in ammunition technology. Some hunters like number 4 shot because it hits a little harder, but the down-

Aaron Phillip Schroder, a professional gun dog trainer and guide at Pheasant Bonanza in Tekamah, Nebraska, leads hunters into the field with his German shorthaired pointer Little Charlie Trouble.

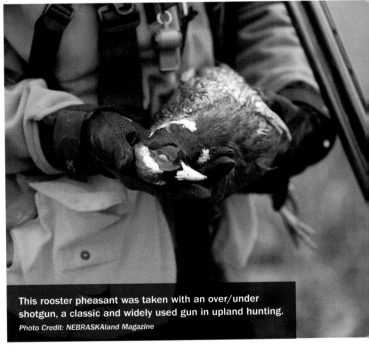

This rooster pheasant was taken with an over/under shotgun, a classic and widely used gun in upland hunting.
Photo Credit: NEBRASKAland Magazine

Hunting chaps help protect your legs against brush, thorns and burrs when hunting for pheasants through thick fields. *Photo Credit: NEBRASKAland Magazine*

side is that you get fewer pellets per shotshell.

For pheasants, 2¾-inch shotshells are suitable; they don't beat up your shoulder unnecessarily compared to magnum loads. But there are times in the late season when birds might flush at longer distances – that's when a 3-inch shell will come in handy. If you are hunting in a federal waterfowl area you will need to use steel shot or other nontoxic shells. In that case, you may want to use 3 or 4 shot. As always, check your local game regulations carefully.

Clothing & Other Necessities

Before you even think about stepping out to hunt, wearing blaze or hunter orange – even if your state does not require it – is a necessity for pheasant hunting. This means wearing orange on your chest, back and head. When the grass is tall, keeping track of your partner or other hunters can be difficult. In the excitement of a sudden flush being aware of your surroundings becomes that much more difficult. A good hunting vest will not only provide you with the compartments you need to hold your birds, ammo, water, snacks and even a small first-aid kit, it will also have enough hunter orange on it so others can easily identify you in the field.

A comfortable pair of waterproof boots is just as important as a good hunting vest. Pheasant hunting is a physical sport that requires you to be on your feet for hours over possibly rough and uneven terrain. Good boots should not only fit well, but also provide good ankle support. Badger holes are a pheasant hunter's nightmare, making twisted ankles and ruptured Achilles tendons serious concerns in this sport.

Every serious pheasant hunter should consider brush pants or hunting chaps that can withstand tough, brushy, thorny vegetation much better than regular pants. Also, dressing in layers is a must when hunting in the fall due to unpredictable weather. Be prepared for heat, cold, rain, snow and wind. Because you will be exerting yourself, cotton should be avoided. It absorbs and holds moisture (sweat) and will make you cold and miserable. Instead, wear fleece or wool, which wick away moisture more quickly and will retain their insulating properties even when wet.

Hearing protection is also highly recommended when pheasant hunting. Do not underestimate the sound of gunfire, which can cause permanent damage to your hearing. Hearing damage can occur at noise levels higher than 140 decibels. Keep in mind that most firearms produce noise higher than 140 dB.

Darlin', a German shorthaired pointer, hunts and trains hard for her owner Aaron Phillip Schroder almost every day of the year.

Water is a necessity for you and your dog. Make sure both you and your four-legged companion(s) stop for a drink and maybe a snack. Even in cold weather you will burn plenty of calories and dehydrate quickly. Be mindful of your dog no matter what the weather conditions might be. By the end of the day they will most likely have traversed twice the distance you have. Since a dog's normal body temperature is higher than a human's, they can easily overheat and fall victim to hyperthermia.

The Hunt Field

Hunting pheasants can be done alone or turn into a group affair, but choose your field wisely. Hunt alone in too large of a field and you'll be chasing birds unnecessarily. But put a large group in too small of a field and things can get downright dangerous. Within a large group of hunters there should be one person that steps up to be the "captain," or the person in charge to make sure that everyone follows all safety rules and to offer guidance to less experienced hunt-

ers. This person is usually the most experienced hunter and most importantly, they should be the most knowledgeable in hunter safety and hunting regulations. Each field has its own nuances; this person should also be able to judge the field conditions before starting.

Usually hunters will line up evenly on one side of a field, abreast, and preferably with the wind in their faces – hunting into the wind gives dogs an advantage in catching the scent of any birds. Always be aware of where everyone else is located when hunting in a large group. This is where the blaze orange comes in handy. Try to stay evenly abreast of each other as you work across the field. Communicate with each other to prevent accidents and always point your gun in a safe direction. Do not shoot too low as a dog or a fellow hunter could end up in your line of sight.

Another way to work a large field is to send some blockers to the other end of the field. Remaining hunters will then move toward the blockers. Sensing hunters closing in, running

When hunting in a large group, walk evenly abreast with other hunters and always point your gun in a safe direction. *Photo Credit: NEBRASKAland Magazine*

pheasants will feel the pinch and be forced to flush instead of running to make their escape. Again, pay attention to where you point your gun and watch for hunter orange.

Field to Table

After a successful hunt, get your birds cooled down and cleaned as soon as possible. Do not leave them to spoil in the back of your truck under the beating sun or sitting in your game bag for long periods of time. Do not let your birds get wet, which can promote the growth of bacteria. We can't say this enough, but tasty meals in the kitchen start with proper care in the field. It's worth it.

Cleaning

There are several ways to clean a pheasant. You can simply breast them out, wet pluck or dry pluck them. Because it is the easiest and fastest way to clean a pheasant, most hunters prefer to breast them out, which requires no gutting. We also usually breast out our pheasants, but we do keep the legs. Although pheasant legs can be filled with tendons, they are great slow-cooked in soups and stews. For a better presentation, plucking a pheasant is preferable, although it is much more time consuming and does require a bit of patience – pheasant skin tears annoyingly easy.

Breasting Out Pheasant

STEP 1. Lay the pheasant breast side up on a flat surface. Pluck a few feathers off the breast to expose some skin. Then pinch or pull the skin apart to tear it, allowing you to pull back the skin and expose the breast.

STEP 2. Continue to pull the skin off the legs.

STEP 3. With a sharp knife, carve out the right and left breasts by following the contours of the pheasant's sternum and ribs, being careful not to puncture through into the body cavity.

STEP 4. Separate the legs by cutting the car-tilage between the ball and hip socket that at-taches the thigh to the back. It helps to bend this joint back. You will hear or feel a crack, which is the femur separating from its socket. Cut off and discard the feet from the legs by cutting the joint where the drumsticks end.

STEP 5. Wash pheasant breasts and legs under cold water to remove any blood and stray feath-ers. Look for any remaining shot pellets and dis-card. Cut off any bruised meat. Dab dry with paper towels and store in sealed bags before cooking or freezing.

Plucking Pheasant

Dry plucking is the most difficult and time-consuming method to clean pheasants, which is why most hunters don't bother with it. But if you're so inclined, start by plucking the back and the wings, saving the breast for last. The breast is the centerpiece of the whole bird so you want to take your time with it. Do not pull, but pluck, anchoring the skin down with the fingers on your opposite hand. Only grab a few feathers

at one time, plucking them with a quick snap-ping motion at the wrist. There are two types of feathers on a pheasant, a light under-feather and a quill-type feather with a stiffer core. The quill-type feathers will give you the most trouble be-cause they can easily tear skin no matter how careful you are. It is important to only pluck one or two of these feathers at a time. They are lo-cated on each side of the breast, on the flanks of the bird and the neck. Afterward, clean the pheasant and cut off its neck, feet and tail.

Wet plucking a pheasant is much easier and more practical. Bring a large pot of water to around 150 degrees – steaming but not boil-ing. Hold the pheasant by its feet and dunk the whole bird into the hot water for 30 seconds. Lift it out, wait until most of the water has dripped off the bird, then repeat twice more so that the bird has been dunked in the hot wa-ter for a total of 90 seconds. Then start plucking the pheasant while it's still warm, starting with the wings, then the difficult quill feathers on the neck, flanks and the sides of the breasts, then fin-ish the rest of the bird. Take your time to avoid tears. Work on only one bird at a time because this method only works while the feathers and skin remain warm. Finally, clean and wash the bird thoroughly.

Cooking Pheasant

Pheasant is one of our favorite meats to cook. Its light meat resembles chicken and it too is versatile in similar ways. It can be adapted into almost any recipe originally made with chicken and can be used in all kinds of cuisines. We've made dishes that range from Indian Butter Pheasant, to BBQ Pheasant Pizza, to Pheasant Coq au Vin, to Pheasant Tortilla Soup.

Frying Pheasant

Frying pheasant breasts requires no special instruction. The only real advice we can give you is that we recommend frying only the breasts, and saving the tougher legs for braising. Pheasant will work great with your favorite fried chicken recipes. They also make tasty pheasant nuggets and fingers – perfect for party appetizers accompanied with your favorite dipping sauces. Fry them battered the traditional way or try Japanese Panko breadcrumbs, which give pheasant breasts a perfect, light crunch.

Roasting Pheasant

Roasting is best reserved for farm-raised pheasants, but it is still possible to roast a delicious wild pheasant. The key to a tender, juicy and flavorful result requires a bit of patience and two important steps: aging and brining. Pheasants are lean birds. Try to roast a whole pheasant without any preparation and you will end up with a dry, flavorless carcass.

Aging allows the meat to tenderize and develop a better flavor. Brining adds more flavor and necessary moisture to the meat. Our friend Hank Shaw, writer of the blog, *Hunter Angler Gardener Cook*, has a great post on hanging pheasant, which requires unplucked, ungutted birds to age in a temperature-controlled refrigerator for days and even weeks. But, we don't

have the space to do that and rarely can we assure that our birds have not been shot in the guts. So, we came up with a way to age a whole pheasant – albeit plucked and gutted – in our everyday refrigerator as shown in the following recipe. After hanging out in our fridge for a week and then sitting in brine, we turned an old, wild rooster into one of the best pheasants we've ever tasted. The meat became more delicate, rich and juicy, characteristics you don't usually get from cooking freshly killed pheasant.

Grilling Pheasant

Pheasant breasts are tasty on the grill, especially after having been marinated. You can grill them with or without the skin. Grill boneless pheasant breasts for five minutes on each side over direct heat, or until just cooked through and no longer pink in the middle. Since pheasant is so lean and can dry out easily, avoid overcooking it on the grill. However, pheasant that has been marinated should give you some room for error.

Grilled pieces of pheasant breasts that were marinated in barbecue sauce. Cut the breasts into small pieces for a delicious pizza topping.

Braising Pheasant

Soups and stews are perfect uses for pheasant legs and even pheasant breasts. The slow, moist cooking method breaks down the tough legs, making them tender and easy to shred.

Aged & Brined Whole Pheasant

Servings: 2
Prep Time: 7-8 days aging,
6-8 hrs brining, 1 hr prep
Cooking Time: 15-20 mins

1 whole pheasant, plucked and aged

1 tablespoon of softened butter

1 teaspoon of Herbes de Provence

sea salt/kosher salt to taste

freshly cracked pepper

quarter of an onion

5 fresh sage leaves, or your choice of fresh herbs

Brine

12 cups of water

¾ cup of kosher salt

¾ cup of brown sugar

optional spices: smashed cloves of garlic, peppercorns, crushed juniper berries, sage leaves, etc.

1. To age plucked and gutted pheasant, pat the bird dry with paper towels inside and out after you've washed it under cold water. Place two layers of paper towels on a plate and lay the bird on top of it, breast up. Loosely cover it with plastic wrap and place it in a refrigerator to help it dry out, about two days. Once dry, replace all the paper towels and seal with new plastic wrap, this time snug to prevent the skin from drying. Put the pheasant in the refrigerator for another five to six days. Replace the paper towels as needed to keep the process sanitary. Average refrigerator temperatures should range 35-40 degrees.

2. An aged pheasant should not smell rotten. Once aged to your liking, make the brine by warming up water, salt and brown sugar in a large pot, just enough so that the salt and sugar dissolve. Add the desired spices and allow the mixture to cool. Once cool, completely submerge the pheasant in the brine. Brine and refrigerate four to eight hours, four hours for a farmed-raised bird and eight hours for a wild pheasant.

3. Preheat the oven to 500 degrees. Take the pheasant out of the brine and allow it to come to room temperature for at least 30 minutes, but no more than one hour before cooking. Pat it dry with paper towels. Stuff the cavity with fresh sage and a wedge of onion. Mix softened butter with Herbes de Provence and rub it on the pheasant and underneath the skin over the breasts. Lightly sprinkle salt and pepper all over the bird. Truss it for more even cooking.

4. Place the bird breast up in a roasting pan. Roast in preheated oven for 15 minutes. Take it out and lower the oven temperature to 350 degrees. Roast the bird at this temperature for 30-40 minutes, or until thigh meat reaches at least 155 degrees. Tent the breast with aluminum foil if the skin starts browning. Rest the finished bird for 10 minutes so it can finish cooking and reabsorb its juices.

The **flavor and texture** of wild pheasant can be greatly improved through aging and brining.

Pheasant Coq au Vin

1. Preheat the oven to 250 degrees. Clean and wash the pheasant thoroughly and remove any fat. Separate into six pieces: legs, breasts and back cut into two pieces. Debone the breasts and cut into small, bite-size pieces. Sprinkle salt and pepper on all sides.

2. Cook the bacon over medium heat in a Dutch oven until it's crispy. Remove the bacon and set aside. Lightly dredge the pheasant pieces in flour and brown on both sides in bacon fat. Set the pheasant aside.

3. Lower the heat to medium-low and add carrots and onion to the Dutch oven. Add more oil if necessary. Add a pinch of salt and pepper, and cook for 10-12 minutes, or until it turns brown, stirring often. Add garlic and cook for one minute. Next, carefully add ¼ cup of cognac to the pan. Scrape the bottom of the pan with a wooden spoon. Place the bacon and pheasant back into the Dutch oven along with any juices from the plate. Add wine, chicken stock, thyme and one teaspoon of salt. Bring to a simmer. Cover with a tight-fitting lid and place in a 250-degree oven for two hours, or until the pheasant is tender.

4. Peel pearl onions and cook them in a skillet with ½ teaspoon of sugar and ½ cup of water over high heat. Cook until the onions start to fry then lower the heat to medium-low. Cook until the onions begin to glaze, stirring occasionally.

5. Heat one tablespoon of butter in a skillet over medium heat. Add mushrooms and sauté for five to 10 minutes, or until browned.

6. Remove the Dutch oven from the oven and bring it back to the stove. Check to see if the pheasant legs are tender. Discard the thyme, then add mushrooms and pearl onions to the pot. To thicken the stew, mash together one tablespoon of flour and one tablespoon of softened butter in a small bowl, then stir this mixture into the stew. Bring to a simmer and cook for 10 minutes. Add salt and pepper, to taste. Serve hot with French bread.

Servings: 4
Prep time: 45 mins
Cooking Time: 2 hrs & 30 mins

3 slices of thick cut bacon, chopped

1 whole skinless pheasant

kosher salt and freshly ground black pepper

½ cup + 1 tablespoon of flour

½ pound of carrots, peeled and cut into 1-inch pieces

1 yellow onion, sliced

2 cloves of garlic, chopped

¼ cup of cognac or brandy

½ bottle of dry red wine, like Burgundy or Syrah (Shiraz)

1 cup of chicken stock

10 fresh sprigs of thyme

2 tablespoons of unsalted butter, at room temperature, divided

½ pound of pearl onions

2 tablespoons of olive oil

½ cup water

½ teaspoon of sugar

½ pound of baby bella mushrooms, quartered

A French classic,
coq au vin or "rooster/cock with wine," is perfect for tough birds like pheasants.

In an effort to curb the rapidly growing population of snow geese, many states have added a conservation hunting season that extends beyond regular duck and goose seasons.

CHAPTER 9

WATERFOWL

Compared to other kinds of hunting, waterfowl hunting is by far the most social one. It's a chance to shoot the breeze with friends, enjoy the smells of bacon and coffee in the blind, compare calls, learn new hunting tips from seasoned shooters and even get in a nap when things are slow. If you're really lucky, the blind will be heated.

Biology

Ducks

There are many species of ducks in North America, divided roughly into the two most common categories: dabblers and diving ducks. Dabblers, or puddle ducks, are those species that lower their heads in the water and lift their tails in the air to feed in the shallow waters they prefer. Dabblers number around 14 different species with the most hunted being the widgeon, black duck, northern pintail, and blue-winged, green-winged and cinnamon teal. There's also the wood duck, gadwall and the most popular duck of all, the mallard.

Although dabblers can submerge their entire bodies into the water, they do not swim deep nor do they stay down for very long. Diving ducks, however, are exactly what their name suggests – diving ducks can dive or swim down to their food. There are 21 diving duck species in North America, including a few sea ducks. The most hunted are the common, red-breasted and hooded merganser, the redhead, the canvasback, the greater and lesser scaup, the bufflehead duck, harlequin duck, ring-necked duck, the common and Barrow's goldeneye, and the common, king, Steller's and spectacled eider. Other differences between dabblers and diving ducks are physical traits to accommodate their contrasting feeding habits, including differences in leg placement, wing size, feather composition and bills.

Geese

North America has around nine different species of geese, depending on whom one asks. Some hunters like to divide the Canada goose into different subspecies. There's also the lesser and greater snow goose, Ross', emperor, barnacle and the white-fronted, also known as the "specklebelly." Among cackling geese, a small-bodied group similar to Canada geese, there are four different subspecies.

Migration

Most waterfowl migrate to find food, better climate and habitat. When their northern habitat begins to freeze and food becomes scarce, waterfowl travel from the northern tundra of Canada and Alaska to as far south as the Gulf of Mexico and beyond. As long as there is food and habitat, birds will stay at their current locations until they are forced to move south as the weather deteriorates. Bird movement and weather patterns are two things that waterfowl hunters closely monitor during each hunting season to determine when to head out to their favorite locations.

Aptly named diving ducks, redheads are easily identified by their bright red head and gray back.

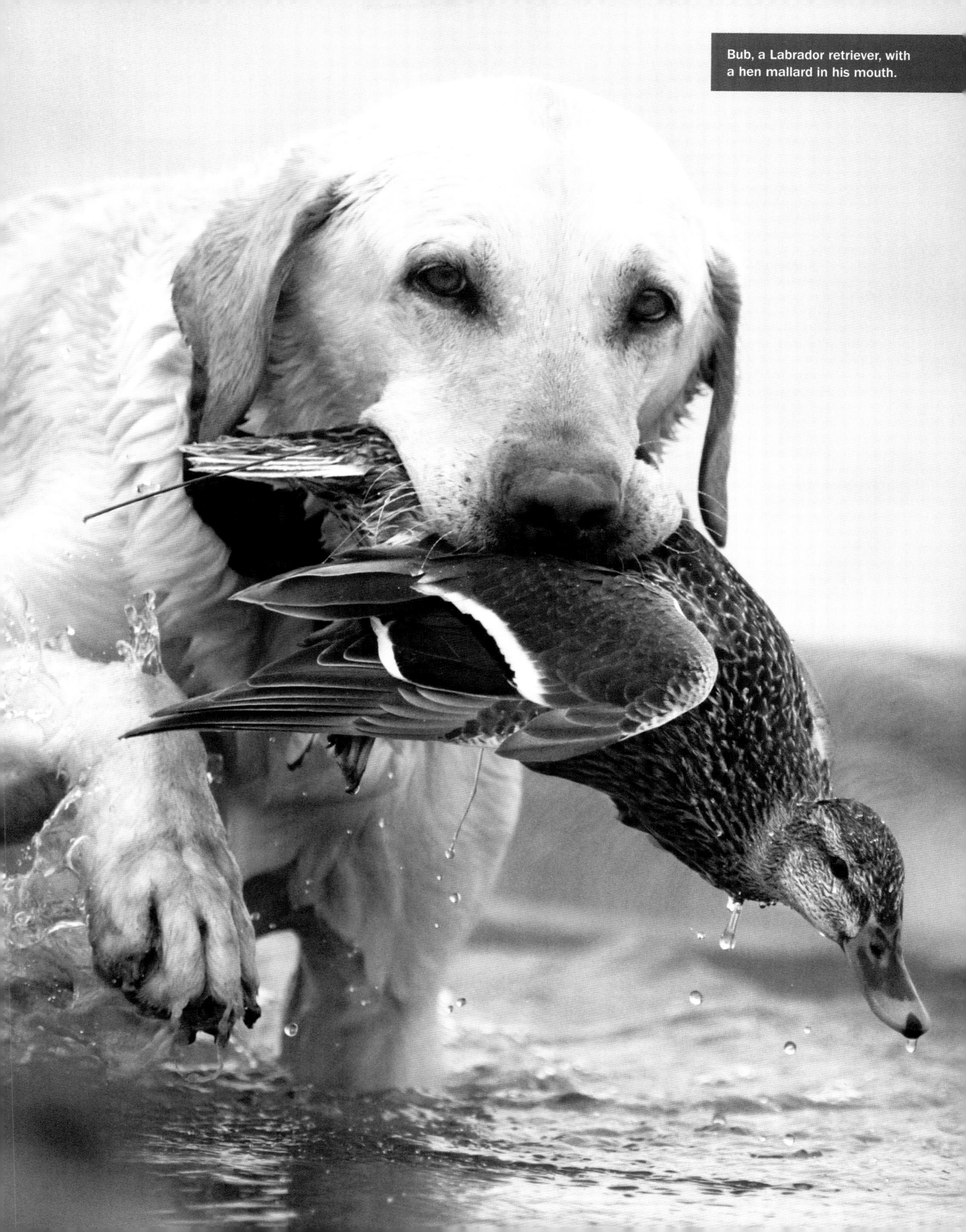

Bub, a Labrador retriever, with a hen mallard in his mouth.

Hunting

Hunting waterfowl can be accomplished over small waters such as ponds and streams, or over larger bodies of water like rivers, lakes and even saltwater bays; hunting on large fields is also possible. An effective waterfowl hunter will know how to properly set up decoys, call in birds, quickly identify birds on the wing, work with a dog, understand waterfowl behavior and be knowledgeable in reading weather patterns and how they relate to bird migration. This may take years to master, and for a new hunter, just wading through duck hunting jargon can be intimidating. If you are a beginner one of the best ways to get started is to find a more experienced hunter and have them show you the ropes. So keep your eyes and ears open – you never know whom you will meet tomorrow. If you have some extra cash, going through an outfitter is perfectly fine.

One of the best first steps you can take is to join Ducks Unlimited (Ducks.org), the world's top wetlands conservation organization. Their website provides a plethora of information about ducks, geese, calling, hunting tactics and more, and also lists local events that will allow you to meet experienced hunters that can help you on your way to becoming a better water-

Waterfowl hunters are early risers, getting up before the break of dawn – which can be the most beautiful time of the day.

fowler. They can also provide you with information on where to hunt. Another great resource would be your local fish and game office. They may be able to provide you with maps and insight on public lands to hunt.

Firearms

The 12-gauge shotgun is the go-to for waterfowlers. All types of shotguns have been used for waterfowling, but the most prevalent is the pump-action shotgun – a solid, simply constructed gun that rarely fails while hunting. Pump-action shotguns are also tough enough to withstand the worst weather that comes with duck and goose hunting, and can hold up to the rough handling of being in and out of the field and a boat.

Semiautomatic shotguns are becoming more popular as manufacturers are designing tougher and more weather-resistant shotguns geared toward the waterfowling community. Over/under shotguns are also popular, but they will only give you two shots when three might be better.

Ducks are tough birds and even though some hunters do it, nothing smaller than the 20 gauge should be used. Some people go with a 10 gauge, but unless you are built like Paul Bunyan, prepare for some teeth to rattle every time you pull the trigger. Plus, ammuniton for the 10 gauge is hard to find and very expensive. When it comes to geese, you can use a 20 gauge but great care should be taken to ensure that the geese are in close range. Aim for the head for a better chance at a killing shot – a hit to a goose's thickly feathered body may not give you the desired result. While a 20 gauge may be fine in some cases, goose hunting is best left to the 12 and 10 gauges. They have enough power to take down these large and tough birds.

Mossy Oak pro staff member Terry Bisgard is ready to grab his shotgun as ducks fly overhead, while his dog Bub focuses all concentration on the sky.

Ammunition

Before going into the details of ammunition, it is important to mention that lead shot for waterfowl hunting was banned nationwide in 1991. This law was passed in an effort to reduce incidences of lead poisoning in many waterfowl species such as dabbling ducks, which were ingesting spent lead shot while feeding in shallow water. Before going waterfowl hunting make sure that you are using nontoxic shot such as steel, bismuth or tungsten, among others. Hunting violation fines can be steep. Always know the rules and regulations in your state and hunting unit.

If you're shooting a 12- or 10-gauge shotgun, "high brass" 2¾-inch length shells do well when shooting ducks over close decoys, but many hunters prefer 3-inch shells, which pack more power and pellets. Some will even use 3½-inch shells, but after a full day of shooting, you will definitely still feel the heavy recoil. If you're shooting a 20-gauge shotgun, a 2¾-inch shell's lighter load will be adequate when shooting at close distances, but the better option is the 3-inch magnum for all-around performance.

Ducks and geese are hardy animals, so stick to larger shot sizes. A popular shot size for ducks is number 2. Shot size number 2 is great for larger duck species like mallards, but for smaller ducks such as teal, shot size number 4 is adequate. BB and BBB are the most popular sizes for shooting geese.

Waders

Waders are essential for waterfowl hunting because they allow you to stay dry while set-

Chest waders are an indispensable tool in waterfowl hunting and will keep you warm and dry during all kinds of hunting conditions.

ting out decoys, positioning a floating blind on the water, wading through mud (and there will be lots of it), getting in and out of a boat, and retrieving ducks. If you're going to hunt flooded timber or don't have a boat or blind, you will more than likely find yourself standing or sitting in pretty cold water. Expect to spend $100–$200 on a good pair of camouflage insulated waders.

Decoys

Waterfowl decoys are man-made ducks or geese, usually made of wood or plastic and often skillfully painted to look realistic. They are set out on water or fields to fool ducks flying overhead to stop and rest or feed, allowing hunters to take a shot once the birds are in range. To finish a flock, or to get birds to commit to your decoys and land, is the stuff of waterfowling dreams.

Seasoned hunters agree that a dozen decoys is a good number to start with, no matter where you hunt. Do not place your decoys too far away to avoid skybusting, or shooting birds that are too far out of range, resulting in wasted shells and wounded birds. Place your decoys within ideal shooting range, which is around 20-30 yards. You will find many brands and types of decoys on the market including the electronic "robo-duck" with rotating wings. Read reviews, do some research and talk to other hunters to decide which decoys are best for you.

Calls

The ability to mimic the sound of waterfowl is an art. It separates the rookies from the experts and requires a certain finesse to be successful. Duck sounds include the basic quack, greet-

Longtime waterfowl hunter Spencer Brooks, from Nebraska, has been hunting since he was 16 years old. Now in his 70s, Brooks is one of the most respected duck callers in Nebraska's waterfowl community.

ing call, feed call, hail call, comeback call, the lonesome hen, pleading call and whistles. All are sounds that can be mimicked with man-made calls, acrylic or wooden instruments that can be manipulated by the user to convince ducks to come closer. The same idea applies to goose calls. Like a musical instrument, not all calls are built the same. They can vary in tone and the one you choose will depend on what sounds best to you. Again, talk to other hunters, read reviews, watch online how-to videos, listen to sound samples of real ducks calling and practice, practice, practice.

Camouflage

Camouflage appears in the form of clothing and blinds to help conceal you from birds. Blinds can be permanent, temporary or able to float on the water. They can sit above the ground or below, and provide room for 10 hunters or just one. Some are simple and others are elaborate, depending on the budget and resources available to the hunter. The most important consideration in blind construction is to make sure that it blends in well with its natural surroundings.

Hunting clothes should also follow the same idea. Stick with drab browns and tan or cam-

Being able to cook and eat breakfast in the blind is definitely a plus while out waterfowl hunting.

ouflage clothing. If you're not in a blind, sit still in places with good natural cover. It's also extremely helpful to cover your face with a camo mask or paint. Waterfowl have keen eyes and your bright face peering through the weeds could be enough to send a flock of birds to the next county.

Retrievers

What on earth could be more excited about waterfowl than waterfowl hunters? If you've ever shared a blind with a Labrador retriever, you'll know what the answer is. Although not required, a good hunting dog can make any hunt much more enjoyable. A good waterfowl dog should be a strong swimmer and able to mark, retrieve and deliver birds to your hand. These are all traits found in the Labrador retriever, which is considered to be one of the best all-around waterfowl dogs.

Field to Table

Caring for waterfowl once they've been shot is no different than any other game. Fortunately, the majority of the season occurs during colder months of the year so heat is less of a problem. Still, remember to field dress ducks and geese as soon as you can.

Labrador retriever Reba showing lots of natural talent at only 10 weeks old. Her owner is Terry Bisgard.

The types of waterfowl you might shoot will depend on what's available in your area. Dabblers like mallards, teal and wood ducks are the best eating, while diving ducks can be slightly "fishy" or "gamy" depending on their diet. Canada geese can be tough but mild tasting, almost like very lean beef, while snow geese can be darker and stronger in taste. Brining is a great option to soften the taste and texture of tough or strong-tasting birds like diving ducks and geese.

Brine for Birds

8 cups of water

½ cup of salt

½ cup of brown sugar

8 juniper berries, slightly crushed

4 cloves of garlic, crushed

5 sage leaves

1 bay leaf

This brine works for any kind of bird. Multiply the ingredients as necessary – you want enough brine to submerge all of the meat. To make the brine, combine all of the ingredients in a large saucepan. Heat the mixture just enough so that the sugar and salt dissolve, then cool completely before adding the meat. Place a heavy dish on top of the birds to keep them submerged in the brine. Cover and refrigerate four to six hours for small birds and overnight for large birds. Keep in mind that the longer you keep the birds in the brine, the saltier they will become. Adjust your seasonings accordingly when cooking.

Cleaning

Waterfowl can be breasted out or plucked whole. After a good day in the field we typically breast out half of the birds and pluck the rest by singeing them with a torch or using wax. You can breast out birds the same way you would with pheasants, or you can try our method, which will allow you to keep its delicious skin. We recommend plucking more mellow-tasting birds like dabblers and Canada geese. For snow geese and diving ducks, your time might be better spent breasting them out without the skin.

Breasting Out Waterfowl

STEP 1. Pluck the feathers off the bird's breast. For ducks, pluck their feathers against the grain. For geese, it can be easier to pluck with the grain. Pluck an area slightly larger than the area of the breast meat. It's okay to have some down left over, but remove as many feathers as you can. We recommend doing this outside and above a trash can to minimize the mess. For areas where the bird has been shot, use the fingers on your opposite hand to anchor down the skin to avoid any tears.

STEP 2. If you decide to keep the legs, which we highly recommend for large birds like geese, pluck all of the feathers off the legs, stopping where the thigh ends or where you expect to remove the leg. The legs can be braised, cooked in a slow cooker and even confit.

STEP 3. Use a small propane torch to carefully singe off the leftover feathers at the exposed areas of the breast and legs. These will burn off very quickly and just a quick pass with the torch will do. It also helps to have someone else hold the bird in place.

STEP 4. Cut out the breasts by following the contours of the sternum and chest. Plucking an area larger than the breasts allows you to keep more of the skin, which will shrink during cooking. Then remove the legs by cutting through the hip joint closest to the bird's body. Cut off the feet from the legs.

STEP 5. Finally, rinse the legs and breasts under cold water. Scrub off any leftover char from the burned feathers if necessary. Dab dry before storing in sealed bags. Discard the rest of the carcass.

Dry Plucking

This is the easiest and fastest way to pluck a whole bird, although it may not be the prettiest. Singeing a bird will often leave little bits of char on the skin and can leave a burned smell on your bird. But for most people this is not a big deal. Always pluck waterfowl before gutting.

Pluck as many feathers off of the entire bird as you can, starting at the wings since they are the most difficult part to pluck. But, you don't have to pluck the entire wing, depending on how much of it you want to keep. Use kitchen sheers to snip off the parts you don't want. Now grab only a few feathers at a time and pluck the back, sides, breasts and legs, which should be plucked against the grain for ducks. We pluck

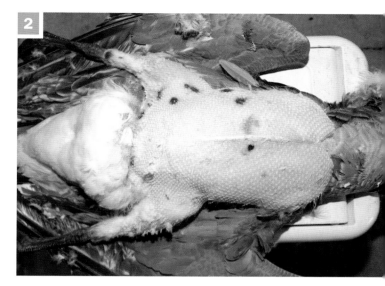

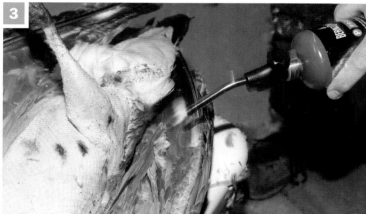

A propane torch is the perfect tool to remove any leftover down from a whole plucked goose.

goose feathers with the grain. The tail feathers should be plucked straight out.

Then hold the bird by the legs and carefully singe off any leftover down feathers with a torch, preferably outside and in a safe location. Finally, cut off the neck and feet with kitchen shears and remove the organs.

Wet (Wax) Plucking

Plucking a bird with wax requires more effort, but the end result is amazing. If done correctly, you will be left with perfectly plucked birds that look like you bought them at the grocery store. The downside, however, is that paraffin wax can get pricey if you have a lot of birds to pluck.

What you need are good kitchen shears, blocks of household paraffin wax (found in the canning section at your grocery store), a sharp knife, a canning pot big enough to fit a duck or goose and a separate container of cold water that's equally large. Wear an apron because it can get messy. We buy wax that is sold in blocks, and the amount of wax that you will need depends

on the size of the bird. A goose will require one whole block and a mallard will require about half of that. You can probably get away with a single block for about three smaller ducks, like teal. When in doubt, err on the side of caution and use more wax than you need. Too little wax will coat your duck inadequately, leaving patches of feathers that won't peel off correctly.

STEP 1. Pour water into the canning pot and bring it to a steamy temperature – you want the water just hot enough to melt wax.

STEP 2. While the water is heating, rough pluck the bird. Do not gut the bird yet. Start by cutting off any broken wings or legs that you're not going to eat, because there's no point in wasting wax on those parts. Then pluck the outer feathers and leave the layer of down underneath; the down is what the wax will cling to, allowing you to cleanly pluck the bird. Additionally, any exposed skin will cook in the hot wax and make your bird look blotchy in the end. Pluck the large wing feathers, which can be tough. The feathers on the chest, back, sides and legs should be plucked against the grain. Pluck out the tail feathers with the grain.

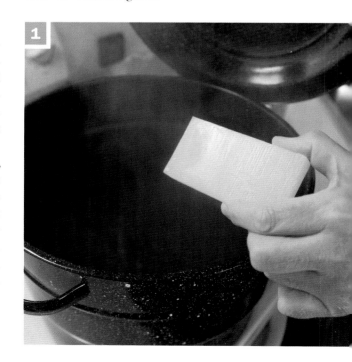

1

STEP 3. Once the water is hot enough in the canning pot, add the wax to melt. Once the wax melts, remove the pot from the heat and place it on the floor, preferably in the garage or outside. Dunk the bird into the pot by holding the head or feet, making sure to get all the body feathers exposed to the wax; the wax will be floating on the surface of the water. Be careful not to get your hands in the wax – it's extremely hot. We like to hold the head in one hand and the feet in the other, then dunk the bird in sideways and turn it to make sure all of it is exposed to the wax. Then dunk the bird into the container of cold water for a few seconds to allow the wax to harden.

STEP 4. After the wax is cool enough to handle, gently use your hands to squeeze the bird, creating cracks to break up the wax casing. Carefully peel off the wax pieces at these cracks, using your opposite hand to anchor the skin down to avoid tears, especially at places with loose skin. Start with the wings because they are the most difficult parts. Peel the breast last because it's where you really want to take your time.

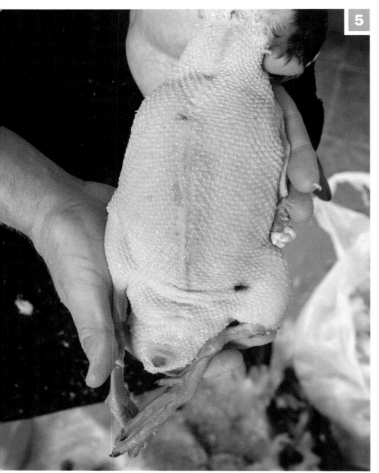

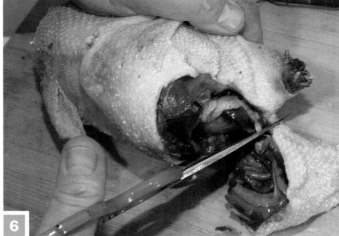

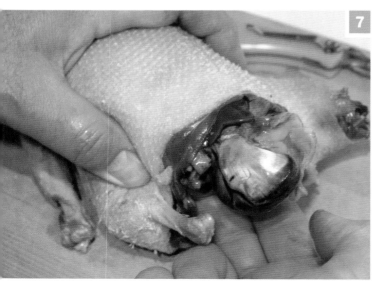

STEP 5. Now you have a perfectly plucked bird.

STEP 6. Use a pair of kitchen shears to cut off the bird's neck and feet. Snip off the wingtips at the second joint on the wing.

STEP 7. To gut the bird, cut off the tail. Reach into the body cavity with two fingers through the cut you just made and feel for the gizzard. Grab the gizzard and pull — it should bring the intestines with it. Next, run cold water through the body cavity to rinse it out thoroughly. Pat dry with paper towels. You can either vacuum seal the birds now, or put them in a covered container lined with paper towels to age in the refrigerator for a few days before freezing. This will help the meat develop a better flavor and texture — the same idea behind aged beef.

Cooking Waterfowl

Compared to other wild game, waterfowl does have a slightly stronger flavor that's hard to describe. Some people like it and others don't, but learning to take care of it in the field and cook it properly will make or break your experience at the table. Like venison, duck or geese should not be cooked past medium or else they will turn into hard pucks that taste like liver.

If you learn to appreciate waterfowl, it can

become one of the best delicacies you will ever have. The rich, sweet fat and distinctly flavorful dark meat will become a taste that you will constantly look for.

Pan Searing Waterfowl Breasts

Just like a good steak, it doesn't take much to enjoy seared waterfowl. All you need is salt and fat to cook it in – the trick is cooking it for the correct amount of time. But before you begin, remember to take your meat out of the refrigerator at least an hour prior to cooking to allow it to reach room temperature and ensure even cooking. Salt both sides well and allow the breasts to sit for about 15 minutes. Pat the breasts dry with paper towels – especially the skin – wet skin does not brown. Score the skin if it's a goose breast or a fatty duck.

Next, add one tablespoon of duck fat, butter or oil to your skillet (not nonstick) and allow it to heat up for a minute over medium–high heat for small ducks like teal, and medium heat for medium to large ducks like mallard. Then lay the breasts skin side down in the fat and cook for three to five minutes for small ducks and five to eight minutes for medium to large ducks (use the recipe on the next page for geese). Flip the breasts over and cook the meat side for one or two minutes for small ducks and three to five minutes for medium to large ducks, depending how you like your meat done. Stand the breasts onto their wide side and cook them for another one or two minutes. Take them off the heat and tent with foil, skin side up. Allow the meat to rest before serving – a couple min-

utes for small ducks and five to seven minutes for large ducks or geese.

Roasting Ducks

Preheat your oven to 450–500 degrees Fahrenheit. Pat a whole plucked bird dry with paper towels and salt the duck inside and out. In a cast iron pan brown all sides of the duck in oil, butter or duck fat over medium heat. Take the duck off the heat. With two celery sticks prop the duck breast up on both sides so that it doesn't tip over in the pan. Place the duck in the preheated oven until its internal temperature reaches 145 degrees. This will take 10-20 minutes depending on the size of the bird.

Grilling Waterfowl

Grilling should only be done with skinless breasts – the grill doesn't do any favors for the skin. Season or marinate the meat as desired and grill it just like you would a steak, but be careful not to cook the meat beyond medium. We like to grill waterfowl to make poppers or filling for spring rolls.

A Canada goose breast that's been salted and scored, and is ready to be seared.

Goose Breast
with Rosemary Fig Sauce

Servings: 2
Prep Time: 5 mins
Cook Time: 30-45 mins

2 Canada goose breasts, with skin

kosher salt, to taste

¾ cup of dry red wine

1 sprig of rosemary

1 teaspoon of balsamic vinegar

3 tablespoons of fig spread
   (we use Dalmatia brand)

1 tablespoon of cold salted butter

Goose breasts are big and thick, making them difficult to evenly cook on the stove. Their fatty skin should be slowly rendered over the stove, then finished in the oven.

1. Preheat the oven to 350 degrees. After cleaning and rinsing the breasts, pat them dry with paper towels. Score the goose skin, but do not cut into the meat. Sprinkle salt to taste on both sides. Lay both breasts skin side down in a cold ovenproof skillet, such as a cast iron skillet. Turn on the stove to medium-low heat and sear the skin side for five minutes, or until it has rendered and is golden and crisp. Halfway through searing, tip the skillet to spoon out most of the rendered fat and save it in a small bowl, but leave enough fat to sear the other sides. Then turn the breasts to the opposite side and cook for an additional five minutes. Next, stand the breasts sideways on their thickest sides and cook for one or two minutes to get some color. Use tongs to hold the breasts upright if necessary.

2. Return the breasts to skin side up in the skillet and gently blot off any excess fat. Roast them in the 350-degree oven for seven to 10 minutes in the same ovenproof skillet or until they reach desired doneness – we prefer medium to medium-rare.

3. Once the breasts are cooked remove them from the oven and onto a plate. Let them rest for five to seven minutes loosely tented with foil. Meanwhile, return the skillet to the stove and turn the heat to medium-high. Add one teaspoon of the reserved goose fat and ¾ cup of red wine. Scrape the bottom of the pan and add the rosemary sprig, then allow the mixture to simmer until the liquid is reduced by half. Discard the rosemary and whisk in one teaspoon of balsamic vinegar and three tablespoons of the fig spread. Allow this mixture to simmer until it thickens. Then remove from the heat and whisk in one tablespoon of cold butter.

4. Serve the goose breasts whole or sliced, skin side up with the sauce served underneath.

Vietnamese Spring Rolls
with Shrimp and Wild Duck

1. One hour prior to cooking the meat, cook the noodles according to their package directions, usually four to five minutes in boiling water. Drain them in a colander and rinse under cold water. Let the noodles stand in the colander at room temperature to allow them to dry.

2. Season the skinless duck breasts with salt and pepper and brush them with olive oil. Prepare your grill and cook the duck breasts to medium doneness. Then boil a pot of water and add the shrimp to it. Boil the shrimp until they're pink and cooked through, about five minutes. Cut the cucumbers into matchsticks and pick mint leaves from the stems.

3. Slice the cooked shrimp in half lengthwise. Then slice the duck thinly against the grain and into small bite-size pieces.

4. Fill a large container with warm or hot water. Quickly wet the spring roll wrappers, shake off any excess water and lay them on a clean, flat surface. When the wrappers are pliable add some rice noodles, cucumbers, duck meat and mint leaves toward the bottom. Add three pieces of shrimp in the middle, with the pink and stripy side down for presentation. Then fold the sides and the bottom over the filling. Tightly roll up the filling.

5. Combine all of the dipping sauce ingredients and mix them well. Serve the rolls with sauce on the side.

Servings: 4
Prep Time: 1 hr
Cooking Time: 5-10 mins

1 pound of skinless duck breasts

5 ounces of fine rice sticks/Vietnamese vermicelli rice noodles

20 raw shrimp, deveined and shells removed

2 small Persian cucumbers (or mini cucumbers)

bunch of mint leaves

14-16 spring roll wrappers

olive oil

salt and pepper, to taste

Dipping Sauce
1 clove of garlic, minced

2 tablespoons of sugar

2½ tablespoons of fish sauce

½ cup of water

1 teaspoon of Sambal Oelek ground fresh chili paste, or to taste

juice of one small lime

Skinless duck breasts
can be grilled, sliced and used for stuffing in spring rolls.

A trio of beautiful, freshly caught and scaled rainbow trout sitting on ice ready to be transformed into a delicious meal.

CHAPTER 10

GAME FISH

Freshwater fishing is one of the most simple and fun ways to get outdoors and bring home some dinner for people all over this continent. There are many species loved by anglers, but we'll focus on a few of the most widespread species available to anglers in North America including bass, crappie, bluegill, carp, walleye, catfish and trout.

Entire books have been written on each of these species and though this chapter may only scratch the surface of fishing knowledge, we hope that it will at least get you started on the right path to a lifetime of adventures on the water.

Bass

Biology of Largemouth & Smallmouth Bass

Part of the sunfish family, there are many subspecies of freshwater bass and the most common are the largemouth and the smallmouth bass. The largemouth originally dominated the southern regions of the United States while the smallmouth bass is mostly found in the cooler waters of the North. Due to transplants, the largemouth has basically spread throughout the country. Largemouth bass tend to be a mottled dark green on the back with light green on the sides and a mostly white belly. Florida large-

mouth bass can reach up to 25 pounds, but in most of their range a 5-pounder is considered a nice catch, and a 10-pounder is a wall hanger.

Smallmouth bass are bronze and brown in coloration on their back with light brown sides and a white belly. Smallmouths don't usually grow to near the size of big largemouths, mostly averaging 1-2 pounds and rarely topping the 10-pound mark.

Bass Fishing Tackle & Tactics

Fishing tackle for largemouth and smallmouth bass are as different as each fish. Heavier tackle is needed for the largemouth as they tend to live in waters with a lot of cover and structure

HUNTING FOR FOOD   **CHAPTER 10: GAME FISH**   **131**

LEFT: Jim Halbrook with a nice largemouth bass at Canyon Lake, California. RIGHT: Jenny Nguyen with her very first crappie, which she caught out of Lake Henshaw in Santa Ysabel, California.

such as rocks, tree roots, fallen trees and aquatic plants. When fishing for largemouths, look for underwater structures where they tend to hide and ambush their prey. Smallmouth bass prefer clear, cool water and less structure, including lakes and rivers with boulders and gravel.

Largemouth Bass:
ROD: 6½-7 feet, medium to medium-heavy action
LINE: 10-12 pound test for densely structured habitats; 8-10 pound test for clear water with less structure
LURES & BAIT: crankbaits, spinnerbaits, jigs, plastic worms, assorted swimbaits and live bait

Smallmouth Bass:
ROD: 6-6½ feet medium to medium-heavy
LINE: 6-10 pound test
LURES & BAIT: similar types of baits and lures as largemouth bass but smaller

If you really get into bass fishing you'll find yourself with several different rod, reel and line combinations set up for special purposes to fish different types of structure.

Crappie

Biology of Crappie

Crappie are also part of the sunfish family. The subspecies are the white and the black crappie. Both can reach 5 pounds, but the average fish will be in the 1-pound range. Although similar in appearance, the white crappie is aptly lighter in color with five to eight vertical bars on its body with scattered speckles of dark green and black scales. The black crappie tends to be darker in shading with much more black on its scales. Minnows are probably their favorite food, so minnow-imitating lures work best when fishing for crappie.

Crappie Tackle & Tactics

A good way to fish for crappie is to drift or slow troll for them. This allows you to locate them in schools as they often move around a lake following baitfish. Crappies like to be near submerged cover such as trees or brush, so use a depth finder to see underwater structures and to find schools of shad, which can reveal where the crappies are. When you find a school cast toward it, and if the fish are in a willing mood you may catch a crappie with every cast. Crappies will also utilize the protection of a boat dock, and if you find them there, it can be a great way to catch a limit without leaving the dock.

ROD: 5-7 feet, ultralight or light action with a light spinning reel

LINE: 4-6 pound or 1-2 pound on an ultralight rod if you are looking for a good fight

LURES & BAIT: 1/64-ounce to ¼-ounce soft plastic tube jigs or curly tailed jigs, Marabou feather jigs (white, yellow and chartreuse are good colors), small minnow, shad and crawfish-imitating crankbaits, live minnow with a bobber

Bluegill (Sunfish)

Biology of Bluegills

Bluegills are mostly olive green and yellowish, and marked by an iridescent blue and purple region on their cheeks and gills. Breeding males are more intense in color, showing bright orange and red on their bellies. They have a tall and flat body with a small mouth on a short head. Also in the sunfish family and related to the bluegill are the pumpkinseed, redear and rock bass, and they all average 7-10 inches in length.

Bluegills are green and yellowish in color with an iridescent blue and purple region on their cheeks and gills.

Sunfish Tackle & Tactics

More people have probably been introduced to fishing with sunfish than any other species. With the proper tackle they put up a great fight for their size, and some fishermen say that pound for pound they are the toughest fighters. For the most part, all sunfish species can be fished with the same gear and tactics, which do not have to be sophisticated. A simple cane pole, line, bobber and hook are all it takes to catch sunfish.

Sunfish can be found in lakes and small ponds, and they tend to spend time near structure and its shade – like weeds, submerged trees or brush, and even under docks. They like shallow water, which makes them a great fish to chase from the shore. Willing biters, sunfish are a great introductory species for kids who are learning how to fish.

ROD: 4- to 6-foot ultralight rod and reel combo; longer and shorter specialized rods are available

LINE: 1-4 pound test

LURES & BAIT: red worms, nightcrawlers, leeches, minnows, crickets and other insects, small spoons and spinners, small crankbaits, mini-jigs, insect imitations and small poppers for fly fishing

Most panfish rods come 4-6 feet long, but some specialized rods can reach out to 9 feet long or more. When starting out go with the tried-and-true method of a simple bobber and hook with a small split shot weight in between.

Walleye

Biology of Walleyes

Walleyes live in rivers and lakes found in cooler climates. A handsome fish, they are elongated in shape with a dark olive back that drops off into a golden color on the sides, and olive bars run down the sides to meet a white underbelly. Their mouths are filled with sharp, needle-

LEFT: Walleyes are one of the best tasting freshwater fish in North America. RIGHT: Rick Wheatley with a perfect eating size 5-pound channel catfish from below the Spencer Dam in north-central Nebraska.

like teeth. Walleyes can grow to over 25 pounds, but a 10-pound fish is exceptional.

Walleye Fishing Tackle & Tactics

Walleyes can be found in both shallow and deep water depending on the time of year; they move up to shallow water to spawn in early spring. Tackle for walleyes can be extensive as there are many techniques used to fool them. Since they can be found at all depths and moods, serious walleye fishermen have many combinations at their disposal. Walleyes are very active at night and many fishermen chase them during low-light hours, bringing even more specialized equipment into the picture. Here is a good starting point for anyone looking to get into some walleye action.

ROD: 7-foot medium-action rod with a fairly soft tip. Choose a rod with a good backbone because you will need the extra strength to set the hook

LINE: 6-8 pound test, a light or clear-color line to avoid the walleye's good eyesight

LURES & BAIT: live minnows, leeches, nightcrawlers, spinners, slim-bodied minnow imitators, thick-bodied crankbaits that imitate shad, leech and nightcrawler-imitating soft plastic swimbaits, spoons, hairjigs and more

To fish with live or imitation bait, attach the bait onto a jighead or on a bare hook with a weight about 18 inches above the hook and below a slip bobber; the slip bobber works great as you can adjust it to the depth where the fish are located. Walleyes can be fished on the bottom much the same way. The jighead may be the most versatile as it can be fished in shallow or deep water. Cast and retrieve the lure with a steady, slow cadence, or bounce it along the bottom.

Catfish

Biology of Catfish

Catfish live in most waters throughout North America including rivers, lakes and streams. The most well-known catfish species are the channel, blue, flathead and bullhead. The blue catfish is the largest of all species, topping the 150-pound mark, and in the old days records show that blues grew much larger in the big rivers of the Midwest. Flatheads can reach 100 pounds while channel cats can top 50 pounds. Bullheads are comparatively small, averaging

1–2 pounds; Washington's state record brown bullhead weighed just over 11 pounds. Catfish species pretty much look similar to one another with beady eyes, elongated smooth bodies and no scales. They are recognized by their catlike barbels (whiskers) around their mouths. Channels are dark gray on top with a white bell, blue cats are more of a bluish gray and flatheads have a wide, flat head and are brown with yellowish sides and brown blotches. Bullheads can be black, brown or yellow.

Catfish Lures & Tactics

Channel Catfish

Channel catfish are the most abundant of the catfish species and are found in many rivers, lakes and streams across North America. They are willing biters and stout fighters when hooked. One of the best rigs to use is a simple sliding sinker rig.

ROD: 8 feet, heavy
LINE: 25-pound line if fishing for big cats, 10-pound line for overall fishing of average cats of 1–5 pounds
BAIT: live bait, dead bait and "stink bait"

Blue Catfish

Blue cats live in large Midwestern rivers along with channel cats. They usually inhabit deep water where channels also live. Blue cats are known for being extremely tough fighters.

ROD: 8 feet, heavy
LINE: 80- to 100-pound test
BAIT: live bait, dead bait and "stink bait"

Flathead Catfish

Flatheads prefer live bait as opposed to dead bait or "stink bait." Considered the tastiest of all catfish, many anglers believe that the flathead's preference for live baitfish is the reason why.

ROD: 8 feet, heavy
LINE: 80- to 100-pound test
BAIT: live bait such as large shiners, sunfish or bullheads; check your state's regulations on live bait usage

Bullhead

As mentioned before, bullheads only average a couple pounds. A good way to fish for them is to use an ultralight rod and reel combo with a sliding sinker rig (see the sidebar on page 136).

ROD: 6- to 6½-foot ultralight or medium rod and reel combo
LINE: 4- to 6-pound test
BAIT: nightcrawlers

Trout

Biology of Trout

There are many trout species, but the most well-known are the rainbow, brown, cutthroat and brook trout. Trout are vibrantly colorful fish that love clear, cold water. They can be found in clear mountain streams, large rivers and even urban lakes and ponds.

Brown trout vary in color, but the most common scheme is brassy brown with dark spots of brown or red, sometimes haloed by bluish white.

Sliding Sinker Rig

Basic but very versatile, this rig can be used to fish for all types of catfish and many other fish. Cut a 12- to 18-inch piece of line off of your main line to use as a leader. Slip a sliding sinker (weight) onto the main line and tie a swivel to the end. Tie your leader to the other end of the swivel and then tie an appropriately sized hook to the leader. The size and type of sinker you use will depend on the water conditions, and the type of hook you use will depend on the bait. Talk to local fishermen to find out what type of setup and bait is best for your area.

The sliding sinker rig works great for a variety of fishing, allowing fish to tug without spooking.

Trout Fishing Tackle & Tactics

As a fish easily raised in hatcheries, trout have been planted all over the continent. Hatchery fish readily take both bait and lures and are relatively easy to catch – perfect for kids and beginners. Wild trout that live in distant streams and rivers, however, can be very difficult to catch as they live on an entirely different diet. The ability to "match the hatch," or know what the fish are eating on any given day is critical.

ROD: 6- to 7-foot ultralight rod and reel combination, or fly fishing gear
LINE: 4-pound test; in heavily fished waters use a 4-pound main line with 2-pound leader
LURES & BAIT: See below

A popular way to fish for trout is by using the same rig you would use for catfish, the sliding sinker rig (see sidebar). Just use an ultralight rod and reel combination with 4-pound test line. In heavily fished waters use a 2-pound test leader on your 4-pound main line to help fool more wary fish. In streams and rivers choose a slightly heavier line because trout will use the current against you. When trolling from a boat, you can also use a slightly heavier setup. It can be very helpful to check with a local fly shop for the best fly fishing setup because rivers and streams vary so greatly across the U.S.

Trout are caught using many different tactics. Minnow-type lures and flashers used when fishing on lakes from shore or trolling from a boat may do well with bigger fish that have been feeding on shad. To fish for trout that are rising and dimpling the surface, fly fishing may be the ticket. Nightcrawlers or mealworms can be especially successful when fishing in small streams and rivers. If you're using a spinning outfit in those small streams, you can also drift your bait downstream to a waiting, hungry fish.

When using a spinning outfit on a small stream, drop your line into the water and float your bait downstream to trout lurking in the best spots.

"Rough fish" that exist in U.S. waters include the (top to bottom) silver carp, river carpsucker, bigmouth buffalo, grass carp, bighead carp and the common carp.

Carp

Biology of Carp

Carp originated ages ago in Asia and Eastern Europe. Though highly regarded in Europe as both a game fish and table fare, carp have never made that distinction here in North America. Considered highly invasive, carp can compromise water quality and push out more desirable native game fish. Several species of carp have made their way into North American waters and the most well-known are the grass, silver, bighead, black and common carp. The common carp is capable of reaching a weight of 50 pounds or more, and when hooked it will put up a fight like nobody's business. Common carp have a strong, stout body covered by large, armor-like golden scales. They feed mostly on water plants but will also eat worms and crustaceans.

Carp Fishing Tackle & Tactics

You will want a strong rod and reel combo when pursuing large carp. The sliding sinker rig used for catfish will work pretty well (see the sidebar on page 136) as carp will drop a bait at the slightest resistance. They also tend to swim in small groups so after you land a fish, get your bait right back out there for another catch. There are no limits on size or the amount of carp you may keep, and they are the perfect candidate for bowfishing. As always, check with your local and state fishing laws for clarification on legal methods of take.

ROD: 6-7 feet, medium action
LINE: 12-pound test, 100-150 yards
BAIT: homemade dough balls, commercial dough baits, corn

Bowfishing for Carp

Bowfishing for carp is becoming a fast-growing sport. Pick up a used bow and attach a reel to hold your line. Then tie a specialized bowfishing arrow to the end of the line. Polar-

The Tramp family bowfishing for carp on the Missouri River backwaters by Ponca, Nebraska. Bowfishing can make for a fun, fast-action day on the water when you find good numbers of carp.

ized sunglasses are a must-have to see fish in the water. Walk alongside the shoreline or wade through shallow water. Once you spot a carp, draw back your bow and aim slightly below the fish to compensate for the refraction of light through the water.

Bowfishing can also be done at night using a boat rigged with bright lights to shine through the water. Check to see if there's a bowfishing club near you to learn more about the sport. If you bow hunt already, bowfishing should be easy to get into and enjoy.

From Water to Table

Place any fish you catch and want to keep on a stringer in the water and alive for as long as possible. Fish will begin to deteriorate soon after they die, so put them on ice as soon as you can after leaving the water. Some established fishing areas have a fish-cleaning station available for your convenience. If not, check with your state's regulations on fish cleaning guidelines.

Fish like bass, crappies, walleyes and bluegills have similar bone structures so they can be filleted the same way. Trout are better gutted and left whole if they're small, but can also be fil-leted if they're larger. Catfish should be skinned and gutted, and can be cut into steaks. Carp can be cleaned several ways depending on what you plan to do with them. Once cleaned, remember to keep fish cold until you're ready to cook it, otherwise freeze it immediately.

Equipment for Cleaning Fish

- ☐ fillet knife
- ☐ cleaning board or table
- ☐ knife sharpener
- ☐ pliers
- ☐ kitchen shears
- ☐ heavy knife for cutting steaks

How to Fillet Bass, Walleyes, Crappies & Bluegills

STEP 1. With a sharp fillet knife, make a long cut behind the gill cover and pectoral fin un-til you hit the vertebrae. Then use the point of your knife and open up the top of the fish by cutting closely along the dorsal fin. When the blade is level with the vent (anus), cut through to the other side of the fish and continue to cut until you reach the tail fin, leaving the skin at the end attached. Be very careful, it can be easy to slip and cut yourself while working on wet, slimy fish.

STEP 2. Go back and continue to fillet the fish from the vertebrae, being careful not to cut through any bones. Follow the contours of the ribs and cut through the skin along the anal fin.

STEP 3. Flip the "flap" of meat over. Using the skin that is still attached to the fish near the tail fin as an anchor, fillet the meat from the skin.

Finally, check the fillet for bones, rinse it with cold water, keep it cold and repeat on the other side of the fish.

How to Clean Trout

STEP 1. Remove the scales by scraping the back of a knife against the skin.

STEP 2. Turn the trout over on its back. Cut the gills free and slice the lower jaw on both sides, but do not completely cut them off the trout.

STEP 3. Cut through the abdomen starting at the base of the lower jaw all the way down to the anus. Then grab the lower jaw and gills and pull the innards out with them.

STEP 4. Scrape out the bloodline along the spine with your thumb. Rinse the cleaned trout under cold water.

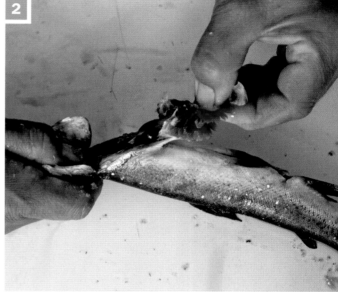

How to Clean Catfish

Catfish Fillets

STEP 1. With the catfish on its side, cut through the skin behind the head. Then cut through the skin along the spine and then along the side of the belly all the way to the tail. With a pair of pliers, grab hold of some loose skin near the head and peel it off.

STEP 2. Now, simply fillet the meat off the ribs and repeat on the other side.

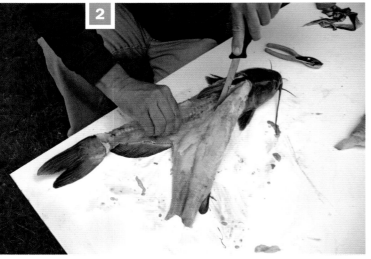

Catfish Steaks

Though not the most common way to butcher fish among anglers, we also like to cut catfish into steaks that can be baked, pan seared, braised or grilled. To turn a catfish into steaks, cut the head off and run your knife down the length of the belly, stopping at the anus. Pull out the organs, then cut across the fish for steaks. Use kitchen shears or a cleaver to break through the thick spine and to snip off the tail.

Nice steaks can be cut from a good-size catfish and cooked in a number of different ways.

How to Clean Common Carp

Unlike any of these other species, carp have two sets of Y-bones on each side in addition to their spine and rib bones. Y-bones are impossible to remove, thus placing carp low on a list of preferred table fare. If scored, however, exposed Y-bones will cook and crisp up in hot oil to become entirely edible. After trying fried carp that is cooked properly, most people will agree that carp tastes just as good as most game fish they've ever eaten.

To clean carp, begin by peeling the skin off with pliers, much like the steps described for catfish. Many species of carp have thick, large scales that can dull your knife if you cut through them, so it's wiser to slip your fillet knife underneath the skin and cut from the inside out. Once skinned, trim off the leftover strip of skin and fins along the top edge and belly of the carp;

you can pull the strips off with pliers, too. Then cut the head off, gut the fish and snip off the tail. Next, score both sides of the fish by making deep cuts along the length of the fish at ¼-inch intervals to help expose the Y-bones to oil. Cut deep enough to hit the spine and ribs, but not all the way through. The top set of Y-bones runs along the entire length of the fish, while the lower set of Y-bones runs from the tail and stops at the rib area. Finally, cut the fish into small pieces. Yes, you are cooking the carp with the ribs and spine still in it, which will keep the fish together despite the scoring.

It's important to score carp before frying to make the Y-bones edible.

When you are ready to fry your fish, make sure to get a lot of batter or cornmeal inside the cuts.

Cooking Game Fish

All of the fish mentioned in this chapter are good to eat. As you may already know, frying is the most common way to prepare fish among anglers. This is no surprise, because few things are better than biting into the combination of a crunchy, well-seasoned batter contrasted by the steaming juiciness of fish inside. For this reason, we are not going to give you a fried fish recipe because we're going to assume that you already know how to stick things in hot oil.

Fish can be fried, baked, grilled, dropped into soups and even braised. The only thing you need to worry about is cooking time, which will vary depending on the thickness of the fish. If the thickest part flakes, it's done. We always bake or grill our fish fillets at around 350 degrees and start checking for doneness after 15 minutes.

Removing the Bloodline

If you or someone you know is extra sensitive to the taste of fish, removing the bloodline will help to improve its taste. The bloodline is the strip of dark, blood-rich muscle found along the center of fillets that often imparts a strong taste to the meat, especially in more oily fish like catfish and carp. Simply remove the bloodline with a sharp knife before cooking, while being careful not to cut off too much white meat. There is little need to do this to mild-tasting fish such as crappies or walleyes.

Vietnamese-Style Catfish
Braised in a Clay Pot

Servings: 2
Prep Time: 30 mins to 1 hr
Cooking Time: 45 mins

1 pound of catfish steaks

4 tablespoons of fish sauce

3 tablespoons of brown sugar

1 inch of fresh ginger, minced

1 large shallot, minced

3 large cloves of garlic, minced

1 teaspoon of cracked black pepper

3 tablespoons of caramel sauce,
   or ¼ cup of water and 2 tablespoons of table sugar

1 green onion, sliced

1 can of Coco Rico coconut soda

1 Thai chili (optional)

1 teaspoon of olive oil

cooked jasmine white rice for serving

1. In a medium-size bowl combine fish sauce, brown sugar, garlic, shallot, ginger and black pepper. Add catfish steaks and marinate for 30 minutes to one hour in the refrigerator.

2. If you can't find caramel sauce in the store, heat one-quarter cup of water and two tablespoons of sugar to a rolling simmer. Mix frequently and wait until the mixture turns a dark brown, but do not burn.

3. Heat the olive oil in a clay pot or thick pan over medium heat. Remove the fish from the marinade and sear for two minutes on each side. Sear it in batches. Then place all of the fish back into the pot. Pour caramel sauce over the fish, then pour in coconut soda to halfway up the fish. Scoop out some of the ginger, garlic and shallot from the leftover marinade and add it to the pot, then discard the used marinade.

4. Cover and simmer for about 30 minutes. Adjust the seasonings with more fish sauce or sugar. Garnish with sliced green onion and Thai chili. Serve with white rice. The catfish skin will soften and become delicious and flavorful.

Catfish steaks
can be delicious braised, as shown in this traditional Vietnamese dish.

Grilled Rainbow Trout
Wrapped in Bacon

1. Prepare your grill to medium heat. Wash the trout thoroughly, then salt and pepper the insides well. Stuff the body cavity with minced garlic and two sprigs of thyme. Lay two slices of lemon and one green onion on one side of each fish and wrap everything together in bacon. This is where a fish basket comes in handy. If you don't have one, secure the fish and ingredients with cooking twine.

2. Oil the grill basket if you're using one, or lightly brush each fish with oil if you're not using a basket. Lay the fish in the grill basket and secure them snugly. Grill them for seven to 10 minutes on each side, or until the bacon is cooked and the fish are flaky. Cooking times will vary. Serve with lemon wedges.

Servings: 2
Prep Time: 10 mins
Cooking Time: 15-20 mins

2 whole rainbow trout

4 slices of bacon

1 large lemon, half of it cut into slices and the other half in wedges

4 sprigs of thyme

2 cloves of garlic, minced

2-4 green onions

salt and pepper, to taste

vegetable or canola oil, for brushing

Special Equipment: fish grilling basket or cooking twine

Small trout are best cleaned whole for grilling, smoking or frying.

The common snapping turtle has a much wider range in North America than its relative the alligator snapping turtle.

CHAPTER 11

TURTLE

Most Americans today could not fathom the thought of eating turtle, let alone believe that it was once a common and highly regarded source of protein up until the 1960s. Turtle meat and turtle eggs showed up regularly on the dining tables of New World colonists and could have very well been served on the first Thanksgiving. By the Revolutionary War, turtle soup became so popular that it showed up on menus and in cookbooks.

It was the centerpiece of wealthy feasts; its preparation difficult and its presentations elaborate. Turtle meat was prized by Great Britain's wealthy from the 18th century on and equally appreciated in the United States. Its status was further elevated in the 19th century and was a must at banquets and elegant dinners. Increasingly expensive and difficult to prepare, few people could aspire to a turtle dinner, which gave way to mock turtle soup, a cheaper version that tasted like the real thing but contained calf's head instead of turtle meat. Turtle soup's popularity carried into the 20th century and made regular appearances at presidential inaugurations and on the first transcontinental trains. It was President William Howard Taft's favorite food.

But by World War II, home cooks grew tired of dressing their own turtles and gave preference to canned alternatives — most notably Campbell's, which often contained no turtle meat at all. By the 1960s turtle soup and the consumption of turtle meat faded into distant memory, except in certain pockets of the United States.

Just think — that ugly, stinky turtle that's been eating the fish on your stringer was at the center of haute cuisine up until only 50 years ago. Don't let their looks fool you. Turtle meat was popular for good reason — it's actually very tasty.

LEFT: Snapping turtles have a powerful beak-like jaw and fast, mobile neck. RIGHT: Snapping turtles have an average lifespan of 30 years in the wild, but some have lived past 75.

Biology

Although many species of turtle can make good table fare, we will focus on the common snapping turtle. Its larger relative, the alligator snapping turtle, only exists in the southeastern part of the United States and is protected throughout most of its range. As we have mentioned before, please check with your state's hunting and fishing regulations before pursuing turtles and any wildlife.

The length of a common snapping turtle's carapace, or upper shell, can grow up to 20 inches when fully grown, though 10 to 12 inches is more common. They average between 15 to 25 pounds in the wild, but can grow much heavier depending on the availability of food. The average lifespan of snapping turtles in the wild is 30 years, but there are some that have lived past 75. Mating season for snapping turtles extends from April through November, with peak egg-laying months in June and July.

Eggs and juveniles are preyed upon heav-ily by raccoons, crows, foxes, herons, bullfrogs, snakes and large fish. But, snapping turtles have few predators once they mature. Since they are too large to hide inside their rugged shells when threatened, a strong, beak-like jaw and mobile neck are snapping turtles' most notable characteristics and best defense tools. They are opportunistic feeders and will consume animals and plants – everything from snails, fish, crawfish, carrion, frogs, other turtles, small mammals and even small birds.

Habitat & Range

Common snapping turtles can be found from the Rocky Mountains to the eastern United States, and from southern Canada to the Gulf of Mexico. They can live in almost any freshwater habitat including ponds, lakes, rivers, streams, creeks, bogs, marshes and ditches. They prefer slow-moving water, however, with soft muddy or sandy bottoms with lots of vegetation. They can also tolerate fairly brackish water.

Snapping turtles can be found in still and slow-moving water with mucky or sandy bottoms and a good amount of vegetation, such as marshes or bogs.

Catching Snapping Turtles

Check your state's regulations for season dates, legal methods of take and bag limits before setting out to hunt turtles. In Nebraska they can be taken by hand, hand net, hook and line, archery equipment, gaff hook or legal trap. In some states, jug or float lines are another legal method of take.

Snapping turtles can be found in almost any freshwater habitat, but you'll have the most luck in bogs and swamps with sandy or muddy bottoms, lots of food sources like carp or frogs, and healthy growths of vegetation like duckweed. During really warm weather sometimes these areas can also smell like rotten eggs, a normal characteristic of wetland habitats. The worse

Impact on Fish & Waterfowl Populations

Snapping turtles are not detrimental to fish populations, despite what many anglers have been led to believe. With slow metabolisms, turtles do not eat nearly enough to impact game fish populations. Studies have also shown that mammalian nest predators and large fish eat far more waterfowl than do snapping turtles. So please, do not kill snapping turtles needlessly. They have been around for 40 million years – since the age of dinosaurs. That is something to respect.

Do not handle a snapping turtle by the tail. Instead, support its weight by holding the shell.

How to Properly Hold a Snapping Turtle

Most people will hold turtles by the tail. For all practical purposes, it's oftentimes the safest and fastest way to get it from the trap to your holding container. However, if handling a snapping turtle for longer periods of time, pick it up by the shell by supporting its weight on both sides with your hands, its head away from you of course. Wearing gloves is a good idea to avoid their sharp claws. For the more experienced, it's also possible to hold the shell by the front and back, with one hand holding the shell right behind the neck and the other above the tail. Do not hold turtles that you don't intend to keep by the tail for long periods of time, this can injure their spine and make it difficult for them to survive after you release them.

You may argue whether this matters with turtles you're planning to kill and eat, but you'll have to purge the turtle for a week before butchering, which we'll cover later in the chapter.

it smells, the better it seems to be for finding turtles.

The methods for catching turtles are variable. It is not uncommon to accidentally catch them while fishing for catfish, and there is no consensus in methodology among those who catch them on purpose. The good news is that turtle hunting is relatively simple and the method you decide to use will be as good as any.

Trapping

Where it's legal, trapping can be an easy way to catch turtles. Traps can be bought or you can make your own, but be sure to check with state regulations regarding trap requirements. Make sure that your trap will allow you easy and safe access to the catch when you want to retrieve it. Bait the traps with pieces of fish, chicken livers, frogs or other bloody pieces of meat by filling a perforated container that you can hang inside the trap. This allows the bait to emit its odors without being eaten too quickly or getting washed away. Place the traps in water 3–4 feet deep near pond inlets or by the banks of rivers and streams. Check your traps the next day, or whatever is allowable in your state. The bait should be renewed after two or three days. When you do catch a turtle wear protective gloves and either grab the turtle by the tail to pull it out, or depending on your trap you can open the lid to gently dump it onto the ground or inside your boat before handling. Transport turtles in large sturdy containers that are tall enough so they can't climb out. When handling, make sure the turtle's head is away from you and from others around you. Its neck and jaw are lightning quick, but the rest of its body is quite manageable.

Hook & Line

Snapping turtles can also be caught with a simple hook and line setup. Large, sturdy hooks especially made for turtles are available on the market. People have caught turtles with a wide variety of methods, but again, it's best to check with your state's regulations first and go from there. The most popular ways to catch turtles with hook and line include trotlines, jug lines or limb lines baited with cut bait, live bait or chicken livers.

A trotline is a heavy line that has baited hooks at even spaces throughout its length, and is secured by a sturdy stump or tree on each end. Hooks are attached off the main line by snoods, or short lengths of line attached to the main line by a swivel or clip. A weight is usually attached in the middle of the main line to keep it submerged. An efficient way to fish, trotlines can be set to cover the width of a river or stream channel. But remember that trotlines are illegal in many states.

Jug fishing is a method of fishing that uses lines suspended from floating jugs or bottles to catch fish and turtles in lakes or rivers; weights can be added to keep the jugs in place.

TROTLINES

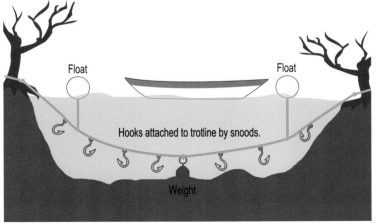

Float   Float

Hooks attached to trotline by snoods.

Weight

Trotlines can be set to cover the width of a river or stream channel. Illustration credit: Ngoc Nguyen

How to Tie a Slip Knot

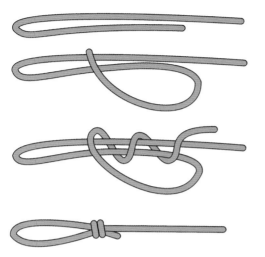

Tie a slip knot 6-8 inches above the hook and bait on a limb line setup; this will help set the hook when a turtle bites. Illustration credit: Ngoc Nguyen

To use a limb line, run one end of your line through a hook and tie a slip knot about 6-8 inches above the hook. The slip knot will allow for give, helping to set the hook when the turtle bites – this also works well for catfish. Then find a tree with a sturdy limb that extends over the water and tie the other end of the line to the limb. Measure your line so that the hook and bait are suspended just below or at the water line.

Remember to always check your lines as often as you can. If you catch something you need to recover it as soon as possible and not let anything go to waste.

Hand Fishing

Hand fishing is how we were taught to catch snapping turtles, though it may require nerves of steel. This method requires a team effort. The number of people involved will depend on the size of the body of water you are on. It also helps to have an extra set of hands just in case the turtle is too heavy to lift on your own. You will need to wear close-toed shoes (old tennis shoes

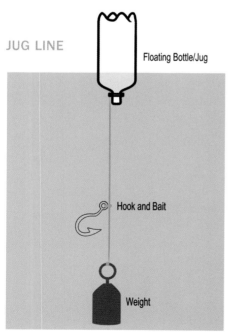

Jug fishing utilizes a floating jug or bottle to suspend the line in lakes or rivers. Illustration credit: Ngoc Nguyen

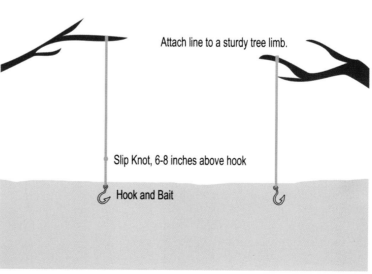

A limb line utilizes an overhanging tree limb to suspend a hook and bait near the waterline. Illustration credit: Ngoc Nguyen

are perfect), and long pants and gloves might be a good idea too. Each person will also need a pitchfork. The person handling the turtle once it's caught will need a large sack to transport the turtle in.

Find a healthy swamp or bog with a sandy or muddy bottom, like those described previously, preferably no more than waist deep. Walking abreast, begin at one end of the wetland and slowly make your way to the other end, using a pitch fork to feel the bottom as you go. Listen for a hard "hollow" sound if you bump something with the pitchfork and feel for movement in the water. If you hear a hollow sound or feel movement, quickly place one foot on top of what would presumably be the shell to keep the turtle from swimming away. If you have an exceptionally feisty turtle you can also have oth-

ers surround the turtle to keep it from escaping. Then slide one hand down your leg and feel for the tail – the shell on the tail end is smoother than by the head. If the tail is curled underneath its body, you will have to pull it away from its body to get a firm hold. Quickly grab the base of the tail, remove your foot from the shell and lift the turtle up and away, preferably with the bottom shell facing you. Or use both hands and grasp the turtle's shell to lift it out of the water. That way you won't injure its spine. Get the turtle to the person on the bank and put it in a sack. This method sounds crazy, but it has worked for many. If it's any consolation, snapping turtles rarely snap at people or other threats when in the water and instead prefer to swim away.

Snapping turtles can also be caught by hand in the winter. If you see one through the ice half buried in mud, preferably in shallow water, chip through the ice and pull it out of the mud. Turtles will be much easier to handle in the winter as they move slower in cooler temperatures.

Field to Table

As rough as they may look, snapping turtles are incredibly delicious. It is said that seven types of meat exist in one turtle, but we think the number is closer to three. Turtles have white meat, dark meat and tenderloin-like meat, which is located on the underside of its upper shell. Undiscerning palates may liken the taste to chicken, but that is not quite accurate. A better description is somewhere between pork and the firmness and bite of alligator meat. Turtle meat is also high in collagen, similar to the meat found in the jowls and hocks of pork. Turtles, like frogs, do have a slight taste of where they were caught – but not in a bad way. Some people say that good oysters taste like the ocean. Well, turtles have a slight hint of "pond."

Turtles can be difficult to clean. Despite turtle meat's popularity in the 18th and 19th centuries it did not survive the movement to packaged, instant foods that changed how Americans

When hand fishing for snapping turtles, pull the turtle out of the water up and away from your body to avoid its jaws.

cooked during the later half of the 20th century. For beginners, butchering a turtle may seem to be a daunting task, but as with anything, practice will make you more comfortable and efficient. Still not convinced? Consider this: a 1-pound bag of store-bought turtle meat could cost you as much as $40!

Purging

Before turtles can be butchered and eaten they should be "purged." According to Nebraska wildlife biologist Ben Rutten, purging allows turtles to empty out their systems, making for a better experience during cleaning. We also think that this helps to leach out some odors that the turtles may have absorbed through their skin while living in swampy, muddy areas.

Once caught, place snapping turtles in a barrel or large, sturdy container. The container should be tall enough to prevent the turtles from escaping and to keep out any curious children or animals. Next, fill the container with just enough water to submerge the turtle(s). Change out the water every few days to keep it relatively clean and remove any feces. Snapping turtles should be allowed to purge for a week before butchering. And don't worry about starving them – snapping turtles have very slow metabolisms and can go for weeks between meals.

Tools for Cleaning a Turtle

- ☐ wooden plank or tree stump
- ☐ two long nails
- ☐ pliers
- ☐ heavy knife for cutting through joints
- ☐ sharp knife for skinning
- ☐ side cutters

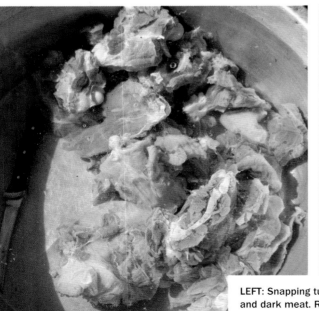

LEFT: Snapping turtles have a combination of light and dark meat. RIGHT: Transport any turtles you catch in a tall sturdy container, like a barrel. You can purge them inside the same container when you get home.

Cleaning

STEP 1. Carefully remove the turtle from the barrel where it's been purging. Flip the turtle on its back and place one foot on top of its underside to keep it stationary. Quickly take hold of its head with pliers by grabbing the upper or lower jaw, then pull out its neck with the pliers (it will try to contract) and cut off its head at the base of the skull. Try not to cut off too much of the neck because that's where the coveted white meat is located. Bury or discard the head as soon as possible — like many reptiles, a turtle's head will continue to bite long after it has been separated from its body.

STEP 2. Cut off the claws at the nearest joint and discard them. Then rinse off the turtle with water.

STEP 3. Lay the turtle belly up on a wooden plank or board. Nail the shell to the board to keep it in place for cleaning; two nails will work fine.

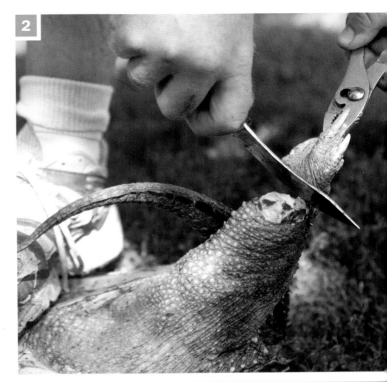

STEP 4. With a sharp knife, fillet the lower shell and as much skin as you can take with it from the body. The lower shell is attached to the top shell on the sides, but it has a soft spot that should be relatively easy to cut through. Then remove the skin from the legs and neck — skin the tail if you think it's large enough to eat. Once the turtle is skinned, remove and discard any visible fat that is covering the meat — it will be yellow and jelly-like. Be careful not to stab any organs, especially the bladder.

STEP 5. Move the organs aside and feel for where the front legs are attached to the shell, then wedge your knife between the shell and the joint and slice it away. Repeat with the other front leg and do the same with the neck.

STEP 6. Move to the back end of the turtle and look for the pelvic girdle, located between the hind legs. With a heavy knife, split this pelvic girdle in half.

STEP 7. Remove the hind legs and trim off any fat. Depending on the size of the turtle you may or may not want to keep a portion of the tail.

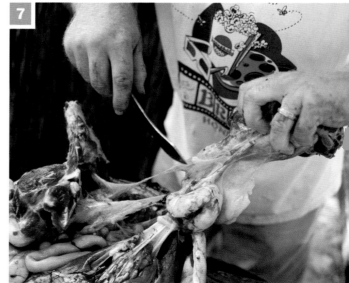

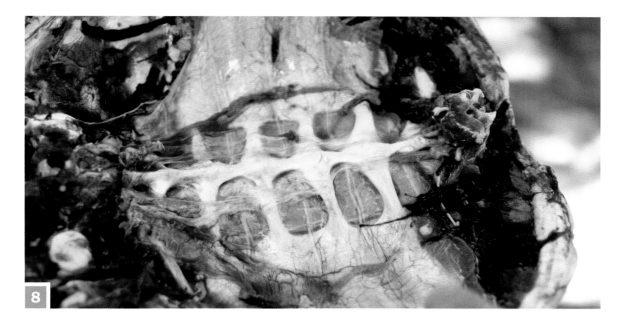

8

STEP 8. In large turtles, remove all of the innards to reveal the spine underneath the top shell. Large turtles will have sizeable meat, or loins, in pockets between the gaps of the spine. To remove the loins, cut out the bony, hard layer on top of the pockets with side cutters and carve out the meat.

STEP 9. Go through the turtle pieces again to remove any leftover skin, fat and visible layers of silver skin. Cut the meat into smaller pieces at the joints. Finally, soak the turtle meat overnight in the refrigerator in a mixture of ¼ cup of kosher salt to every four cups of water. You can also soak the meat in your favorite brine for a different flavor. In addition to taming any off-taste that may still exist in the meat, this soak or brine will add flavor and help to keep the meat moist when you're ready to cook it.

Cooking Snapping Turtle

Turtle is a game that has reached both the highs and lows of culinary fashion. Those who remember its history can still find highly coveted turtle soup at some restaurants in New England, and it is still a specialty at a few Creole restaurants in the South. But among most modern-day hunters and Americans in general, turtle meat does not even exist in our consciousness as something that would be desirable to eat. Consequently, very few turtle recipes exist.

What knowledge we do have on cooking turtle, we owe to the Ruttens of Boone County, Nebraska. They invited us out to their annual family turtle hunt and gave us a crash course on how to clean and cook them. We learned that snapping turtles are best cooked slowly at low temperatures, steamed or simmered in soups and stews. We were also told that turtle meat should not be grilled or fried without being parboiled beforehand. This is because fresh turtle meat, especially that of bigger, older turtles, will become tough and inedible when using quick, hot cooking methods such as grilling or frying.

Cook It Slow: Steaming & Soup

Steaming, braising and making soup are the most ideal ways to cook turtle. As mentioned before, turtle meat can be very tough, but treat it right by cooking it low and slow and you will end up with tender, juicy and flavorful meat. The first turtle meat we tried was fried and then steamed, and it was fall-off-the-bone tender. Our friend Kim Rutten gave us the recipe on page 159 that was passed down from her parents.

Thai-Style Turtle
and Potato Curry

Servings: 4-6
Prep Time: 20 mins
Cooking Time: 2 hrs & 30 mins

1 tablespoon of oil

15 Baby Dutch yellow potatoes, halved, or 2 medium russet potatoes, peeled and diced

half an onion, chopped

1 (14 ounce) can of unsweetened coconut milk

2 tablespoons of yellow Thai curry

2 bay leaves

fish sauce, to taste

1 pinch of sugar

zest of one lime or lemon

chopped cilantro for garnish

cooked jasmine rice
   or bread for serving

Turtle Stock
1½ pounds of turtle meat on the bone

4 ribs of celery, chopped

1 carrot, chopped

1 yellow or white onion, quartered

6 cups of water

1 whole stalk of lemongrass

1. Combine the turtle, celery, carrot, quartered onion, water and slightly bashed lemongrass in a stockpot. Bring it to a simmer (never let it boil), then cover and cook for 1½ hours. Once tender, remove the turtle pieces from the pot and pull the meat from the bones. Set the meat aside. Strain the stock and discard the spent vegetables and set aside.

2. Put the potatoes and a pinch of salt into a pot and cover with water. Parboil the potatoes until they're just tender, but not cooked all the way, then drain.

3. In a wok, heat the oil over medium-high heat. Add the chopped onion and sauté until it's translucent, about five minutes. Lower the heat to medium, then scoop out the top thick and creamy layer of coconut milk from the can and add it to the wok. Allow the coconut to liquefy and bubble for a couple of minutes, then add the yellow curry and stir.

4. Add the rest of the coconut milk, turtle meat, potatoes, bay leaves and enough turtle stock to cover all of the ingredients. Keep any leftover stock on hand to loosen up the soup later, if needed. Stir well and bring to a boil. Then simmer for 30 minutes to allow the ingredients to marry. Add lime zest, fish sauce and sugar to taste and remove the bay leaves before serving. Ladle the soup into individual bowls, sprinkle cilantro on top and serve with jasmine rice or crusty bread.

For those with sensitive palates, **this savory & spicy soup** will hide any "gamy" flavors snapping turtles may have.

Fried & Steamed Turtle

1. Preheat the oven to 250 degrees Fahrenheit. Rinse the pieces of turtle meat under cold water and pat dry with paper towels. Then lightly sprinkle salt over the pieces – don't overdo the salt if the meat has already been brined. Heat 1 inch of oil in a frying pan over medium-high heat, then lightly dredge pieces of meat in flour and fry them until they're golden brown on both sides. Drain on paper towels.

2. Place the browned turtle pieces in a large oven bag, or two if you have smaller bags. Pour in the wine or water, then close up the bag according to the package directions. Place the bag in a baking dish to keep it upright and to catch any leaks, and cook in the oven for three hours at 250 degrees. Garnish with fresh parsley before serving.

Servings: 6-8
Prep Time: 15 mins
Cooking Time: 3 hrs & 30 mins

3 pounds of turtle meat on the bone, cleaned and cut into small pieces

all-purpose flour for dredging

kosher salt, to taste

vegetable oil for frying

1/3 cup of dry white wine or water

fresh Italian parsley, chopped

Special equipment: large oven bag

Fried turtle must be steamed afterward to make the meat moist and tender.

Bullfrogs are the most typical frog species caught for consumption in the United States.

CHAPTER 12

FROG

Frog legs are a delicacy and eaten in many parts of the world. They are most notable in Chinese and French cuisines, but also appear on menus in Vietnam, Thailand, Indonesia, South America, parts of Europe and in the American South. We can attest to its popularity in Vietnam after spending three weeks there and seeing it on almost every restaurant menu. Mild and tender, frog legs taste like a cross between chicken and fish, and they can still be found in some grocery stores. Fry or sauté them in lots of butter, and you can never go wrong.

Though considered more of a Southern tradition in the United States, we'll have you know that frog hunting is a lot of fun. When it's the middle of the summer and the days are hot, it's nice to have a reason to steal away into the cool night air, armed with giant flashlights, fishing poles, nets or spears.

Biology

Among those who hunt and eat frogs, bullfrogs are the most targeted species for consumption due to their size and availability. They are the largest of all frogs in North America, reaching up to 8 inches in length and weighing up to 1½ pounds. Bullfrogs can be easily identified by their tympanum, or circular eardrums, located on both sides of their heads. The upper surface of their bodies is typically green and mottled with gray-brown. Their belly is an off-white color, blotched with yellow or gray. The eyes are prominent with brown and yellow irises and almond-shaped horizontal pupils.

Bullfrogs prefer warm, humid weather and will bury themselves in the mud to hibernate during the winter. At first, the call of a male bullfrog can be mistaken for cattle. Its deep "baarrrrummpph" grumbling can be heard for long distances.

A well-known fact about bullfrogs is that they will eat almost anything they can fit into their broad mouths including insects, mice, fish, birds, snakes and even other frogs.

Bullfrogs are typically a green color with gray-brown mottling on the upper body, and they have very prominent eyes.

Range & Habitat

Bullfrogs are found throughout the continental United States and their range extends from Nova Scotia, Canada, to as far south as Mexico and Cuba. They can be found in freshwater ponds, lakes, rivers, streams and marshes.

Frog Hunting Equipment

There are several ways to catch bullfrogs. Some people catch them with a fishing rod, others by frog gig (spear), some with their bare hands or with a net. When fishing for frogs choose a short rod like an ice fishing rod, for easier maneuvering in the reeds. Choose 6- to 8-pound line and any type of soft, plastic worm-type lure no longer than 3 inches in length.

Frog gigs or spears can be bought for less than $10. Attach it to a long, sturdy handle such as a bamboo or pine dowel, or even a broomstick. Note that not all states allow gigs as a legal method of take.

The most important piece of equipment, however, is a bright, powerful light, preferably a headlamp that allows both of your hands to be free. This light is used to mesmerize and blind the frog, allowing you to get close enough to catch it.

We also recommend taking a cooler, stringer, waders, a bug-free headnet and lots of bug spray.

Hunting

Hunting for frogs is fairly simple provided that you know where they are. Once you have found a good body of water where you know

LEFT: Entice a hungry bullfrog by dangling and wiggling a soft, worm-type lure in front of it. RIGHT: Bullfrogs can also be caught by hand and net, and it's a lot of fun to try!

eating-size bullfrogs live, arrive just before sundown so you can get a good look at the lay of the land; though bullfrogs are active during the day and night, they are easier to find in the dark. Walk along the shoreline or wade in shallow water after the sun goes down. You can also travel along the shore in a small boat, canoe or kayak. With your light and keen eyes, search for frogs hiding among the reeds and behind fallen logs and limbs. Once you spot one, keep your light on the frog and inch close enough to dangle and wiggle your lure in front of the frog for it to grab. When the lure is in its mouth, set the hook and hopefully you've just caught a frog.

If you try a frog gig, get close enough to strike and use both hands for accuracy. If you're catching frogs by hand or net, it's best to hunt with another person – one person can hold the frog's attention with their light while the other person comes from behind to catch it.

Always check your state's game and fish regulations before hunting frogs. Note that some states do have bag limits, length requirements and restrictions on legal methods of take for bullfrogs. For example, gigging is not allowed in some states.

Field to Table

Once caught, bullfrogs can take a long time to die. If piercing them in the head doesn't work, try forceful blows on the head against a hard surface. Rinse them off to get rid of any pond scum and then store them on ice until you can clean them.

Cleaning

STEP 1. With kitchen shears or a sharp knife, cut the skin around the frog's "waist" just above the legs.

STEP 2. Snip off the feet.

STEP 3. Anchor the frog's body with one hand, then grab the skin on its back with pliers. Pull the skin down and remove it from the legs.

STEP 4. Snip off the legs at the "waist" and trim off any organs that are still attached. Split the leg pairs in half for easier cooking and eating. Rinse them under cold water and pat dry with paper towels before freezing or cooking.

Cooking Frog Legs

Frog legs are fairly simple to cook and they taste mild, somewhere between fish and chicken. The best ways to cook frog legs are to fry, sauté or grill them. There are even recipes where they are used in soups and stews, though we have never tried it.

Already very tender, frog legs don't need to be cooked slowly or marinated. Just season and cook them through with your method of choice. If you took care of them properly in the field they should not taste fishy or off. The following recipe is one of our favorites and uses a combination of frying and sautéing.

Chinese-Style Frog Legs
with Ginger & Scallions

1. Heat ½ inch of oil in a frying pan over medium-high heat. Lightly salt the frog legs and then dredge them lightly in flour. Fry the legs in batches until both sides are browned. Drain them on paper towels.

2. Pour out the oil from the pan and clean out the pan. Add one tablespoon of butter and sauté the scallions, garlic, jalapeno and ginger for one or two minutes, or until fragrant and toasty. Add ¼ cup of water and bring it to a boil. Then add the white pepper, sugar, soy sauce and cooking wine, and bring the whole mixture to a boil.

3. Return the frog legs to the pan and toss with the sauce. Garnish with cilantro. Serve by itself or with white rice.

Servings: 2-4
Prep Time: 10 mins
Cooking Time: 30 mins

24 frog legs (12 frogs)

¼ cup of flour

vegetable oil for frying

1 tablespoon of butter

4 scallions, chopped

3 cloves of garlic, minced

1 jalapeno, chopped

1 tablespoon of ginger, minced

¼ cup of water

¼ teaspoon of ground white pepper

1 teaspoon of sugar

2 tablespoons of soy sauce

2 tablespoons of rice cooking wine

chopped cilantro for garnish

In addition to **French cuisine,** the use of frog legs is also very popular in Chinese cooking traditions.

There are over 300 crayfish
species in the United States.

CHAPTER 13

CRAYFISH

Crayfish came to us in the form of "Viet-Cajun," a Vietnamese and Cajun fusion crayfish boil that swept Southern California several years ago. No longer an exclusively Southern delicacy, it was suddenly cool to eat crayfish and restaurants like the Boiling Crab made Los Angeles and Orange County news headlines. Copycats began popping up all over the city. Lines went out the door. People couldn't get enough of those little lobster-like crustaceans tossed in garlicky, spicy butter. But unlike lobster, crab and shrimp, crayfish are widely found in the United States, even in the Midwest. You don't have to live near the coast to enjoy this great-tasting shellfish.

Biology

Also known as crawfish, crawdads and mudbugs, crayfish average 7 inches in length and resemble small lobsters. To the untrained eye they may all look very similar, but North America is actually home to over 300 species. The greatest numbers are found in the southeastern part of the United States where they are used as bait to catch fish and also widely eaten by people in the form of crawfish boils, étouffée and gumbo. Crayfish can also be found in the Pacific Northwest, Midwest and Southwest. They are nocturnal but can also be active during the day. Much like their saltwater cousins, the lobster and crab, crayfish are good scavengers and will feed on plants, worms, insects and eggs from fish and frogs.

Range & Habitat

Crayfish can be found in a variety of freshwater habitats including rivers, streams, pits, ponds, natural lakes, drained canals and reservoirs. They prefer rocky areas where they can hide from a long list of predators that includes raccoons, snakes, possums, large shorebirds and large fish like bass, catfish, walleye and even trout.

Crayfish can often be found burrowed into the mud near shallow water, hence their nickname mudbugs.

Catching Crayfish

Look for crayfish during the warmer months of the year when they are most active between April and October. The easiest and quickest ways to catch large quantities of crayfish for eating are by trapping or dip nets. Other equipment you may need are buckets, bait (if using traps), a cooler and chest or hip waders. To trap crayfish, use a specialized crayfish trap or a minnow trap with a larger opening. These can be round or square wire boxes with openings that allow the crayfish to enter but are difficult for them to exit. A trap door that will allow you to easily empty your catch is a must. Use a dead fish or even a can of dog or cat food to bait the trap. Poke a few holes in the can to allow pieces of the pet food to escape and attract crayfish. After baiting, tie a rope to the trap and toss it into a rocky area to settle onto the bottom. Tie the other end of the rope to a tree and let it sit for a few hours or overnight. Do not leave traps unchecked for too long, especially if they are completely submerged in the water because crayfish will drown. Most states allow the use of multiple traps, but check your local game and

One of the easiest ways to catch crayfish is to use baited traps.

fish regulations first.

Another way to fish for crayfish is by using long-handled minnow dip nets, and this is where waders come in handy if you don't want to get wet. With a dip net in hand, walk along shallow areas while dragging your dip net along the bottom to catch any crayfish on your path. Lift your net every once in a while to see if you are successful. Keep a bucket nearby to hold your catch.

If you only need a few crayfish for fishing and not for eating, a fun way to catch them is

Long-handled minnow dip nets are also useful for catching crayfish in shallow water.

Do not submerge crayfish when transporting or storing them – they can drown.

by using a fishing rod and a small piece of hot–dog. To do this, locate a crayfish under the wa–ter, then carefully drop your bait down to the crayfish and wait for it to grab your bait. When it latches on to the hotdog, slowly but steadily raise the unsuspecting crawdad to the surface and quickly flip it into a bucket.

Crayfish can also be caught by hand, but this can be painful if done incorrectly. Search the shallows and look under rocks. When you locate one, quickly grab it behind the head so it cannot reach back to pinch your fingers. This tactic will be easy once you get the hang of it.

From Water to Table

Carry a bucket or have one nearby as you fish to keep your catch in while you work. Pour a little bit of water into the bucket to keep the crayfish from drying out, but do not submerge them – crayfish will drown if they are not al–lowed to come to the surface to breathe. After you are done fishing, gently put your crayfish into a large cooler. Pour a little bit of water into the cooler. Again, do not submerge the crayfish and give them some room so that they can crawl on top of each other to get some air. Transport them with the cooler cracked open.

When you get home you will need to wash the crayfish to remove mud and grit. Pour more water into the cooler, stir the crayfish around and then drain the cooler. Repeat until the water is clear. You can cook the crayfish immediately or keep them alive until you are ready to cook them. To keep them alive, simply keep them in the cooler with a little bit of water. Depending on how many crawdads you have, you may also want to separate them into more coolers to reduce their stress. Crayfish are best kept alive at temperatures between 40-50 degrees Fahrenheit. We were able to achieve this by leaving the coolers outside overnight in October. Keep the lids open and try to cook crayfish within the same day. Do not leave them in direct sunlight.

Some people will purge crayfish by soaking them in salt water, but we have found that this does not make a difference – you will still have to devein them later on if clean tails are what you're looking for. The salt will also kill the crayfish, requiring you to cook them immediately.

Cooking Crayfish

There are two basic ways to cook crayfish – cook them to serve whole, or cook them to use the peeled tail meat in other dishes. Since there are plenty of Louisiana crawfish boil recipes available online and in books, we will show you a few different ways to prepare your crayfish: how to cook and serve crayfish whole Vietnamese-Cajun style, how to peel and save the tail meat to use in other recipes, and how to make stock from the shells. Before cooking your crayfish, however, sort through your bucket or cooler to discard any dead ones.

How to Cook Crayfish Whole

Eating whole crayfish is a tradition for many. It's a meal reserved for close friends and family who are not afraid to eat with their hands and get a little messy. If you have newcomers over for dinner don't forget to give them a little coaching – it's the proper thing to do as the host. Plan for 1-2 pounds of crayfish per person.

TOP: Crayfish will turn bright burned orange or red when they are cooked. BOTTOM: Boil crayfish in batches to keep the water temperature from dropping too much and to allow for accurate cooking time.

1

To eat whole crayfish, break off the head and then peel the tail. If you twist off the end of the tail correctly it may pull the sand vein out with it, which can be gritty when eaten. Some people will also suck out the contents of the head, which contains the greenish colored tomalley, or liver, that's actually quite tasty.

How to Boil & Peel Crayfish for Other Uses

STEP 1. Bring a stockpot of water to a rolling boil. Add the live crayfish and boil for seven to eight minutes then check for doneness. Cook them in batches to keep the water temperature from dropping too much. Add more water to the pot as necessary as you work.

STEP 2. Once the crayfish are cooked, snap the head and tail apart. Toss the head into another container to save for stock.

STEP 3. Use kitchen shears to cut along the top of the shell, which also opens up the meat underneath to reveal the sand vein for removal. Deveining crayfish is optional, but often desirable. Toss the meat into another container.

STEP 4. Refrigerate the tail meat if you plan on using it soon, or freeze it in vacuum-sealed packaging to be used later in soup, gumbo, jambalaya, mac and cheese, for frying, etc. Place the shells (heads, claws and tails) into a zip-lock bag and freeze to be used for stock.

Butter, Garlic & Cajun-Spiced Crawfish

1. Bring a large stockpot of water to a boil. Juice one lemon into the water and add the spent lemon into the pot. Once boiling, add the live crayfish and cook for seven to eight minutes in batches. Peel one crayfish to check for doneness and allow the cooked crayfish to drain in a colander.

2. Meanwhile, heat three sticks of butter in a medium-size saucepan over medium heat. Once melted and heated, add the minced garlic, paprika, Old Bay, cayenne, black pepper, basil, seasoned salt, juice from half a lemon and honey. Heat this mixture for about 10 minutes at a simmer, or until the flavors are well incorporated. Be careful not to burn. Taste to check seasoning.

3. Once all of the crayfish are cooked and drained, toss them into the sauce. Serve them with chopped cilantro garnished on top. To stretch the meal even further, toss in some steamed corn, boiled potatoes and sausages.

Servings: 2
Prep Time: 20 mins
Cooking Time: 20 mins

3 pounds of live crayfish, washed and rinsed

3 sticks of unsalted butter (1½ cups)

1 head of garlic, peeled and minced

1 tablespoon of paprika

2 tablespoons of Old Bay Seasoning

½ teaspoon of cayenne pepper

¼ teaspoon of cracked black pepper

½ teaspoon of dried basil

¾ teaspoon of Lawry's Seasoned Salt

juice from half a lemon, plus 1 lemon

1 tablespoon of honey

chopped cilantro for garnish

Vietnamese-Cajun
style crawfish that are boiled and then tossed in a garlic butter sauce.

Crawfish Bisque

Servings: 4-6
Prep Time: 30 mins
Cooking Time: 1 hr & 30 mins

1 pound of cooked crayfish tail meat, peeled and deveined

3 tablespoons of butter

1 large yellow or white onion, chopped

1 cup of carrots, chopped

1 cup of celery, chopped

6 cloves of garlic, minced

5 tablespoons of tomato paste

5 tablespoons of flour

6 cups of crawfish stock or seafood stock (see next recipe)

½ cup of cream sherry

1 teaspoon of smoked paprika

2 sprigs of fresh thyme

cayenne pepper, to taste

kosher salt, to taste

¾ cup of heavy cream

chopped parsley or chives for garnish

cracked pepper

1. Melt the butter in a large stockpot over medium-high heat. Add the onion, carrots, celery, garlic, a pinch of salt and sauté for five minutes or until the onions turn translucent. Then add the tomato paste and sauté for one or two minutes, being careful not to burn the paste. Next, sprinkle the mixture with flour, then stir and sauté for one minute.

2. Add the crawfish stock, cream sherry, paprika, thyme and cayenne. Cook for 30 minutes over medium-low heat, stirring occasionally to keep the bottom from burning.

3. After 30 minutes or when the veggies have softened, discard the thyme. Then transfer the mixture into a blender and pulse until it's smooth. Do this in batches to avoid any splatter. Return the blended soup into the pot and season it with salt to taste. If the soup is too thick, thin it out by stirring in more stock. If you don't have any more crawfish stock then chicken stock is okay.

4. Stir in heavy cream and check the seasonings again. Keep the crawfish tails whole or give them a rough chop. Ladle the soup into bowls and garnish with crawfish, parsley and cracked pepper. If desired, sauté the crawfish in melted butter to warm them up.

Crawfish bisque is a creamy soup made with tomato, vegetables, sherry, crawfish stock and heavy cream.

Crawfish Stock

Heat one tablespoon of oil in a stockpot. Add the celery, carrots, onion, a pinch of salt and sauté for five minutes or until the onion turns translucent. Then add the crawfish shells and sauté for another two minutes. Add water into the pot as well as fennel, bay leaves and juniper berries. Cover it and simmer for 30 minutes. Then take the stock off the heat and steep for 10 minutes. Finally, strain the stock through a fine mesh strainer. Cool and refrigerate the stock, or freeze it if you don't plan to use it relatively soon.

Makes 2 quarts
Prep Time: 5 mins
Cooking Time: 40 mins

1 tablespoon of olive oil

4 ribs of celery, chopped

2 carrots, chopped

Half an onion, quartered

1 quart of crawfish shells

2 bay leaves

2 quarts of water

1 teaspoon of crushed juniper berries or whole peppercorns

4 fronds of fennel

A savory stock
can be made from the shells of
cooked crawfish and vegetables.

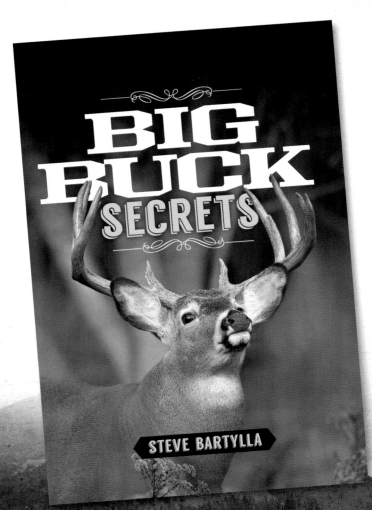